the lost diary

By David P. Mancini
24th Division, 19th Infantry

the lost diary

ISBN:0-9778389-0-0

Designed by Manuse Design, Inc.

*This book is dedicated
to my loving family.*

Thank You

To my squad – family and dearest friends –

Joe Manuse, a longtime friend, my golfing partner, art director and designer of this book. Mary Clark, my dear friend who edited, pulled together and typeset my hand-written notes. My son Bob Mancini, who paved the way for this book to be published because he was a believer. My son Dave, who wrote the epilogue. The contributions of my brothers and sister. Much gratitude to Rori Murrell, CSW, ACSW, Readjustment Therapist at the VA, who helped me in my personal battle with PTSD. She encouraged me to put my experiences on paper as therapy. This was an effort of my extended family, because without their encourage-ment and support I never would have gotten through it.

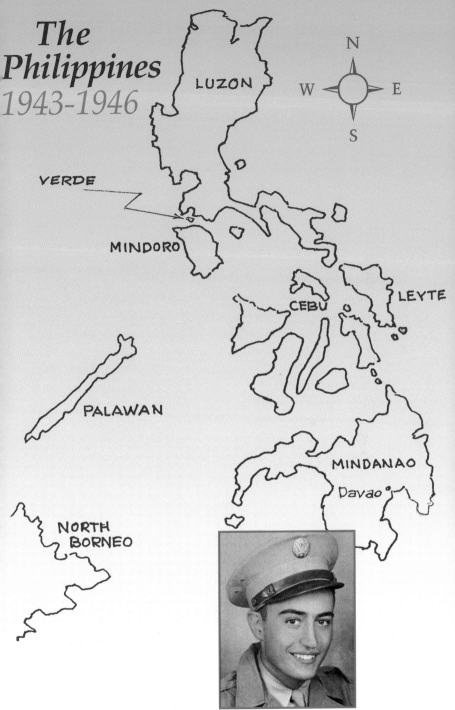

The Philippines
1943-1946

LUZON

N
W · E
S

VERDE

MINDORO

CEBU

LEYTE

PALAWAN

MINDANAO

Davao

NORTH
BORNEO

Pfc. David P. Mancini

the lost diary

VIGNETTES OF A WORLD WAR II COMBAT SOLDIER

24th Division, 19th Infantry

★ ───────────────────────────────

F O R E W O R D

I am writing this book from memory because my original diary was lost. Some of my original sketches are included, as I had sent them home in letters to my family. At 80 your mind becomes a bit like your eyesight. Events become unfocused. It's too bad we can't have bifocals for our minds. Forgive an aging GI for inaccuracies of memory, but I have tried to put down the events exactly as they happened. I met people who blessed and saved my life, and others determined to snuff it out.

This is my memory, my time, my World War II diary.

David P. Mancini

─────────────────────────────────

Prologue

My parents grew up in Campolemisi, a small village in Tuscany, north of Lucca in the Apennine Mountains. It was a village of not much more than 100 people. At the time, there was no electricity, telephone or radio, so news traveled by word of mouth. Homes were lit with oil lamps. It was a humble and rustic life. Some of the houses had a barn attached. In cold weather the villagers depended on the heat from the animals, added to that of the fireplace, to warm their homes. The village had a church, a school, my grandfather's flour mill, and a *bottega*, which was actually a little restaurant where young people gathered. The bottega was a center for discussion of politics and current events, for dancing and little flirtatious affairs. The ladies of the village would wash clothes at a large communal well called *il pozzo*. Because the surrounding mountains were snow-capped all year round, fresh water steadily ran off the steep mountains, constantly replenishing il pozzo. At the well, the ladies exchanged the latest town gossip, and if anyone had come up from Florence or Pisa, they would share news from the cities.

Mama was one of eight children, four girls and four boys. They were very poor in comparison to my father's family. My maternal grandfather was a cobbler. He was a kind-hearted man, and often people took advantage of his kindness and didn't pay him. It was left to my grandmother and their daughters to visit his debtors and collect the money.

My father's family lived in a modest home, but my grandfather owned a flour mill and sawmill. There were six children. One brother was a *carabinieri* (policeman) in Milan. Other brothers had emigrated to Argentina. There was one girl, and an older brother who died at 17. My father was the youngest, and when he was born he was given the name of his brother who had died, Danielle. He and his older brother, Guido, were the first to come to America in 1909. My father was 17 at the time, and didn't speak a word of English.

Papa was a true breadwinner. He was a man's man and not afraid of work. He was stocky, 5' 9" tall, and over 200 pounds. His legs were like tree stumps. He had power-ful hands with long, strong fingers. His thick wrists were twice the size of most men's. I never met another man who lived life with such excitement and enthusiasm. His first job in America was as a dishwasher and clean-up man at a restaurant in Rochester, New York. His work experience there was miserable. As an immigrant, he was tormented constantly. Harrassed and humiliated, he suffered much anguish. Unfortunately, the head waiter wanted to get a job for one of his relatives. Knowing that my father didn't understand or speak enough English to defend himself properly, the waiter created a situation that caused my father to be fired. This was Papa's first taste of American justice.

He served his adopted country during World War I and told us about defending his name during basic training. He was bullied at Fort Dix and arrested after pounding the offender who called him a "Wop." Brought up before the officers' board for a court martial, he proclaimed in his broken English, "When I was drafted into this army my name was Danielle Mancini, not Wop. And if anyone calls me that again, I'll send that man to the hospital, too." The charge was dismissed. He served in France as the mess sergeant of Company E, 310 Infantry Division. His mess kitchen traveled by horse-drawn wagons with the infantry during the battles of Verdun in 1917 and 1918. As a result of his active service, he became a naturalized citizen on June 5, 1919 and was hon-orably discharged from the service on June 6, 1919.

Mother was a Madonna. Beautiful. Her name was Ancilla. She was 21 when she sailed with her sisters on the ship to America in 1918. She traveled in steerage (below deck in the cheapest passenger accommodations). One officer, the captain of the stewards, would bring her extra food because he wanted to date her. She didn't want anything to do with him, but she played along just to get the extra food for her sisters.

In Italy, Mama had been warned to stay away from Danielle and not become involved with him in America. My father had a reputation as a womanizer. Of course, when she finally met him — a rugged, blonde, blue-eyed, handsome man — she fell in love with him. To dispel the rumors and show her how nice he was, Papa went to church with her every Sunday while he was courting her. As they began to get serious with each other, he brought her his paycheck. Papa worked a lot of overtime, and all the money went to her. He cooked for private parties, worked at a factory making wooden boxes, and would do just about anything to make extra money. When they had reached their goal of saving $1,000, they married because now he had proven himself.

The first Sunday after they married, my mother got ready to go to church and said, "Danielle, get ready, we'll be late for church." He looked at her and said, "I don't go to church." She said, "You've been going to church with me every Sunday for the last year." "That's because I wanted to marry you," he replied. "I don't go to church. The church is *tutto una fantasia* (it's all a fantasy)." She was devastated. Although he wouldn't attend a service, he would walk her to church and then go back home.

We were poor growing up. Born in 1924, I have vivid memories of the Great Depression. Papa worked on the night shift for wealthy people at the Genesee Valley Club, and for George Eastman, founder of Eastman Kodak. They knew he had four children and allowed him to bring food home. So although we didn't have much money, we always had more than enough food on the table. The money he earned went to pay for our housing and clothing, and my parents even managed to save a modest sum. With his overtime and special parties that he worked, we had a comfortable life despite the Depression. Papa worked long hours to take care of his family. My mother was the one who really raised us. She was better educated than my father; she finished sixth grade, the equivalent of junior high school in America. She taught us to love opera and the arts.

Campolemisi

Trout stream that operates the mill.

My father's house. Renovated by my cousins.

My son Bob and I, at *il pozzo*.

She would quote from *The Divine Comedy*, Boccaccio's *Decameron*, and other great literature. She talked to us about Greek history, and how Garibaldi united Italy. She brought culture to us and held the family together.

My mother was very frugal. But she was convinced that education was the key to a good life, and she was determined to send all of us to college. She said, "Education opens all doors." My mother handled the money, and she sacrificed everything to save for our education. When my sister graduated from high school and got her first job, she took Mama to her first movie and bought her first pair of silk stockings. Papa bought his first car when the government finally declared a bonus for World War I veterans. It was a 1934 Ford and he paid $700 for it. That was his pride and joy. He only drove it in warm weather, and stored it in winter. Eventually, when the neighborhood teenagers discovered he was ready to trade it in, they bid on it because it was in mint condition.

I am sad for our weak young men of today who have to rely on welfare. There were no such words in my parents' vocabulary as "handout," "welfare," etc. My father's motto was, "A day's pay for a day's work." He taught us that if you were hired for 50 cents an hour, you gave your employer a dollar's worth of work. He was always proud to say that no one could ever complain about his ability to produce. This was his badge of honor and he wore it with pride. My father was also an honest and loyal man. He never betrayed a friend. It was unthinkable to do so for any reason. Papa protected his family name with passion. Never dishonor your name. He told us, "I don't have much to give you except my name." He taught us to always keep our word. Your word is your passport through life. In the 45 years that I had the honor to know him, he never broke a promise. His word was as good as gold. Many young people today seem to have lost the sense of honor and pride that was such a part of this adventurous immigrant.

Rochester, New York – My Family

I remember that day in August of 1943 when I left for the Army, along with other guys from my neighborhood. At the train station everyone was hugging and kissing and crying. The whole neighborhood was there, even people who didn't have children of their own to see off. There were a lot of false smiles as our families and neighbors tried to make us feel better. In my memory the sounds amount to a tearful silence.

I was a senior at East High School in Rochester, New York, and America was at war. School wasn't important to me anymore, and I was drafted into the Army before I could complete my senior year. I had mixed emotions; I wanted to defend my country, but not to destroy my family. Of course, they wanted to keep me safe at home.

My father had served in World War I as an American soldier. He was a youngster when he came to America from Italy at 17, and about six years later the war broke out. He served in France, and was on the front lines in the Battle of Verdun. He knew all too well what war was all about. When I left for the Army, my father was at the train station with my family to see me off. He was a very strong man in many ways, physically and emotionally. He rarely showed his feelings, but he gave us a lot of love. When we were saying goodbye as I boarded the train, he started to cry. I had never seen my father cry. He said to my mother in Italian, "He's too innocent, too young to go. He may be 18, but he's so naïve and innocent, he's no more than 14 or 15." While I was away, my mother was my last thought before I fell asleep. I could always picture her face and feel my father's embrace. I remember learning later that my father was depressed for weeks. He very seldom smiled, and my mother was devastated all the while I was away. The impact on my parents was so evident in the first package of pictures I received when I was in New Guinea. My brothers and sister were smiling at the camera, but my mother looked like she was shrinking away. My father looked so sad.

In 1945 when I was wounded in the Philippines, I had surgery in the field hospital, and a few days later a chaplain came by to help me write a letter home. I had made a vow to myself that I would never tell my family what I was really doing, so I wrote to tell them that I was slightly wounded and I was fine. In fact, I called it a "million dollar wound" because I would be home soon. The War Department had already notified my family that I had been wounded. Unfortunately, an eager reporter from the Rochester *Democrat and Chronicle* went to my house with a photographer and notified my mother that they had received information that I had been killed in action. They were looking for a picture of me and they wanted to take a picture of the family for the newspaper.

My parents were shocked. They couldn't believe it. They knew I had been wounded, but thought I hadn't been seriously hurt. My mother kept saying, "I have this telegram saying he's alive." The reporter went back to the paper to check it out, and eventually returned to say there was an error. In the meantime, my parents assumed that maybe I had died from my wound. My poor mother never recovered from the shock of hearing that I was dead. Later she told me, "I died for a while." The doctor said that the shock aggravated the effects of her arthritis, and shortly thereafter she became a semi-invalid. She wore leg braces for the rest of her life. Fortunately, my letter eventually arrived by V-mail and they learned I was alive.

People don't understand that war touches people far from the front lines. They don't realize the catastrophic effect war has on families and loved ones. There's a domino effect. It starts with the person who is leaving and then continues right through those who are left at home. To have my mother suffer so, devastated me. A simple mistake by an overeager reporter affected my mother's life forever. She never really recovered from the shock and had difficulty experiencing true joy after that day. There was a permanent sadness in her face.

I learned recently from my brother Bill how affected he was. After the family waved goodbye and my train left the station, he and my youngest brother, Joe, walked home together, sobbing. Bill was 15 years old at the time. He still remembers a man saying to him, "Don't worry, kid. He'll be all right. He'll be back." ★

The following story is my brother Joe's memory of that day.

The Other Battlefield

By my brother Joe Mancini

Little did we know what was in store for us that day in June of 1945, as my mother, sister, and I went about our usual routine. I was 16 years old at the time and I remember, like other families in the neighborhood, the patriotic gesture of displaying the American flag in the front window to signify that a family member was in the service. Our flag honored my brother Dave, who had been fighting the Japs in the jungles of the Pacific.

My thoughts of Dave were interrupted by the sound of a car pulling up to the front of our house. A young lady with a pensive look stepped out and approached the side door. I didn't know what to make of the very somber look on her face. Little did I suspect how this stranger was about to alter the serenity of that day.

She immediately identified herself as a reporter from the local newspaper, then asked if our house was the residence of David P. Mancini. I informed her that it was, but that Dave was presently serving in the Army. She asked to speak to either my father or mother. My mother then came from the kitchen to see who was asking for her.

The reporter hesitated before she spoke, then proceeded to explain that she was writing an article about servicemen killed in action and needed information about the death of my brother Dave. Her revelation was devastating! My mother held onto me for support; the shock quickly drained all color from her face. My sister Clara, overcome, slumped into a chair.

Regaining enough composure, I exclaimed, as I was fighting back tears, that what she had said could not be; Dave was wounded in action. We had a telegram to prove it. Grasping for words, the reporter apologized and conceded that perhaps she had made a mistake. She promised to go back to the news desk to clarify Dave's status and return as soon as possible. She hurried off, visibly shaken.

The element of uncertainty made the hours waiting for her return seem like an eternity. Our family had gone through enough hell with the months of worry and concern for Dave's safety and well-being, and now this!

As promised, the reporter did return. We were waiting at the side door just as she had left us – stunned. As she approached the house, her demeanor said it all. Our Davey was alive! ★

Epilogue: Some memories never fade.

Camp Upton, Long Island – The Assignment Center

On the train to Camp Upton, I thought about home and how I had such a wonderful time growing up in an Italian-American family. We had a large family, and there was a lot of love, laughter, and fun. We got together for an extended family party every week, and laughed and sang and danced.

Now here I was listening to this sergeant barking at us as if we were cattle. It was like a door had slammed shut in my face. I was thinking that we're not even in battle and already they have destroyed our freedom. You're treated like you're the lowest man on the totem pole, and every day was the same monotonous routine. As soon as we boarded the train in Rochester, someone was in charge, barking orders and hollering. Not that I expected to be greeted with flowers and music, but I had thought there would be an adjustment period. Not so. They just throw you in and lock you down, and you're there for the duration.

I was lucky that a kid who grew up in my neighborhood was on the train with me. Joe Mortellaro was a couple of years older than I. He took me under his wing and brothered me until we left Camp Upton. Joe was a religious sort. He couldn't stand the things they had us do. The rules were so ridiculous – like bouncing a quarter on your bed to test that you'd pulled the bedding tight enough. We resented the fact that they treated us like children, and wound up pulling KP for five days because we talked back. During our assignment at Camp Upton, Joe and I met Moe Cohen, who became my lifelong friend.

Camp Upton was a revelation for me. Raised with a religious Catholic background, I was shocked at the first VD film showing we were required to attend. It confirmed all the teachings of the nuns – not only the terrible sins you were committing with sex, but also the retribution –

unbelievable disease and pregnancy. Although we grew up with strict rules and precautions about sex, because so much emphasis was placed on how sinful sex was, it had the effect of making us think more about it. If you were adventurous you challenged authority, and there were many in our neighborhood gang who experimented. The nuns had unknowingly opened a whole new world for some of us.

Back home, I was taught to be very modest. The humiliation of squatting in front of a dozen soldiers was embarrassing. With no privacy it was difficult to "go." I was constipated for a few days until the morning prunes took effect. Discussing this with Joe Mortellaro, he enlightened me on the facts of life. He told me, "Don't let this bother you. Before it's over, you'll probably shit in the woods and howl." I found it incredible that there were separate toilets designated for the guys with VD and crabs.

After about a week I discovered that the boisterous, tough guys, no matter where they came from, were not as tough as they made themselves out to be. The quiet, more sensitive, and reserved guys often proved to be the better soldiers. ★

Camp Upton – Meeting Moe Cohen

Moe Cohen was the most relaxed soldier I ever met. I can honestly say that Moe helped me to survive basic training with his street smarts (he grew up being persecuted because he was Jewish), his humor, and his cavalier attitude toward military authority. You would have to search far and wide for a friend as true. Moe loved his family and his friends. He was not the ideal barracks soldier, but in combat he could make John Wayne look like a dud. I was blessed that he took me under his wing. He taught me to ignore the chickenshit and to pay attention to what mattered to survive. For instance, he showed me how to sneak away and get into the officers' mess. We'd pretend we were working on tables, and we got good meals. It wasn't long, however, before our caper was uncovered.

Moe grew up not far from me, on Kelly Street in Rochester. It was a tough neighborhood populated by a mixture of Italians, Jews, and blacks. Moe went to Franklin High School, a rival of my own East High. Although he didn't play sports in high school, he was fast and well coordinated. He was about six feet tall with dark hair and a rugged build. He was a tough Jewish boy from the other side of the tracks who looked like Anthony Quinn.

"Being with Moe was like being with family, and that hasn't changed in over 60 years."

On our way from Camp Upton to basic training at Camp Croft, South Carolina, Moe arranged for us to sleep on our duffle bags. (Much more comfortable than sleeping on crowded seats, like cattle.) He kept my spirits up and encouraged me to be more assertive. At some point he nicknamed me "Davinko." Physically, basic training was not difficult. I was in great shape and could handle anything they threw at me. But emotionally I felt isolated, deceived, and disillusioned by the prejudice of my fellow soldiers. Moe attracted controversy, largely because he was Jewish and wouldn't take shit from anyone. On many occasions, for example when we got into arguments, I would be asked what I saw in "this kike." Of course, that doubled my fury and started another confrontation. I'd tell these guys that Moe was more man than any of them ever would be, and they couldn't kiss his ass on their best day with the sun shining.

We were required to take IQ tests, and received our assignments based on the scores. Unfortunately, Moe was assigned to Communications, and I was in Intelligence and Reconnaissance, so we were separated. During basic training, I always looked forward to seeing Moe and we would get together whenever we could. When I laid eyes on him it was like bringing me closer to home. Being with Moe was like being with family, and that hasn't changed in over 60 years.

We learned that our parents were in contact to exchange news of what we were doing, and to reassure each other that everything was fine. When we were in combat we were in different battalions, but would always write home reporting on whether we'd seen each other. We had a pact. Regardless of what was going on, we'd always say, "I saw him and he was doing well." This way, when our parents compared notes, they were always reassured. Of course, it was all a big scam. When I got wounded we were toast because Moe had just written home that I was fine.

I was so occupied while I was away, it never occurred to me to think of myself as suffering. But I was determined, at all costs, to avoid having my family suffer. I went to such lengths to protect them from the real horrors of war. They never received anything from me to make them suspicious about my activities. I sent them cartoons and funny pictures, and joked about Army life. I never mentioned any incidents of war. I only told them stories of seeing Moe and having our laughs together.

It was bad enough when I had to write home that I was wounded, and they received a telegram from the government. Then a blundering reporter, driven by a media determined to sensationalize our plight for the satisfaction of its readers, destroyed all of my efforts. Everything I did to spare them was blown away by this individual. Knowing my family so well, there had to be a tremendous amount of hurt and suffering.

As my brother said, my family was on their own battlefield. ★

Camp Croft – Basic Training – Night March With Percussion

In boot camp we sometimes went on forced night marches. We had to carry a full field pack that was quite heavy. I learned from some of the older vets that they would take butt cans, roll them up in a bundle, and replace the heavy equipment in their pack. I decided to give it a try. The pack looked nice and neat, but it was light.

Although Moe was in another part of the camp in a communications outfit, a forced march was a group affair so we often marched together. I decided one evening to tell Moe about my newly discovered field pack trick. He thought it was a great idea but said, "You SOB, why didn't you tell me!"

Moe got behind me in line. He was walking back there with his rifle slung over his shoulder, and he started bringing the butt up and hitting my cans so they would go "bing... bing..." I told him, "Moe, cut it out! The goddamn sergeant will wise up to what I've done!" He was laughing. He thought it was funny. After our first few miles, the sergeant was going up and down the line and he said, "What the hell have you got in there, Mancini?" He pulled me out of line and checked my pack and discovered the butt cans. He told me, "You finish this march, and if you think you're going to get away with something, you're going back out again with the next section tomorrow night, you wiseass."

> "What the hell have you got in there, Mancini?"

I figured that I was going to pull this second forced march. They were pretty brutal with a full field pack. Moe felt sorry because he'd gotten me into trouble, so he hatched a plan. We would fall out, roll over in the ditch, and let the rest of the group march off. Then we'd go back to camp and sleep it off, and when the others came in, we'd join them for donuts and coffee. And that's exactly what we did. On our first break when it was dark, we were near a bunch of trees. I rolled over on my back along the side of the road and kept quiet, and Moe went along with me. The rest of the platoon left and we hightailed it back to camp. We were in our bunks sleeping when I heard the group coming back. We slipped out and fell in at the back of the line and got to enjoy our donuts and coffee.

The sergeant came up to me and said, "Don't forget, you're coming back in with a full pack and I'm going to check it out." So the next evening I went up to him. He checked me out but then he said, "Go back to your bunk, you little shit." He let me off, and I didn't have to do that second march. ★

Camp Croft, South Carolina – Hand-to-Hand Combat Training

One day we had combat fighting. They lined us up ten to a side, facing each other. The instructor would blow a whistle and the recruits on either end would rush to the center and attack each other. There were certain moves and holds that we had to learn before we got into combat. We were expected to use every hold possible to down our opponent. In fact, they expected us to hurt each other if we could. We were taught to go for the "family jewels" and for the throat and nose. Our sergeant would yell, "Go for the family jewels, choke the shit out of him!"

I was small, but very agile. Usually I could hold my own for at least two rounds. The rough part of the whole thing was that if you beat your opponent, as soon as the sergeant blew his whistle, the fight was over and we would quit. The next man in line would charge out and no matter what position you were in, even if you were on the ground, he would attack you. You had to fight your way out of it. I was pretty proud of myself because at 135 pounds, I was significantly outweighed in most cases and yet there were times when I went up against as many as three opponents straight, and I won. It probably shocked some people that I was pretty tough for my looks. At that point I didn't shave. I still had peach fuzz on my face, and not very much of that. I was often questioned about my age. They doubted I was old enough to be in the Army. Sometimes I'd be identified as "that baby-faced kid." Consequently, I soon got the nickname "Baby."

Playing Paratrooper

Some of the basic training we received seemed like a piece of cake – until that dreaded day. We were assembled in one of our Intelligence and Reconnaissance rooms and told that we were going to learn how to fly. This was Army intimidation. The corporal in charge proceeded to tell us

13

about parachute drops. In our case, it seldom happened in combat, but it was possible that the occasion would arise where we would have to drop in to get information on enemy troop movements. First, we learned to jump off a four-foot platform, hit the ground, and roll. With much cursing, we practiced until we could all tumble to their satisfaction.

Now came the next step. They marched us over to a very high platform. It probably was only about 60 feet tall, but I swear it was more like 100 feet. We were instructed to follow a sergeant up a very narrow ladder to the top. The platform seemed very small and some of us were skittish about standing near the edge. Being afraid of heights, I was especially terrified. I remember looking down. The ground seemed miles away. I thought I would crap my pants, especially when the corporal demonstrated how to harness up and jump.

Of course, it was perfectly safe, but talk is cheap and when we went through the actual exercise, it was pretty scary. For me, the most frightening part was climbing up the ladder and standing on that open platform. My legs were rubbery and

Staff Sergeant Biggs

it felt like a good gust of wind would blow me off. When I secured the harness and hooked up to the rig they had set up, I felt safer. The rope was attached to the platform on one end, and to the ground on the other. You had to build up your courage to leap out over the edge and have trust and faith in the harness. From that height, everything on the ground looked tiny. We each had to jump three times.

14

The best time to introduce somebody to the training for war is when they're young. In your youth, you think you're invincible. You don't analyze anything too much. And you don't want anyone to think you're a coward, so you just obey orders because it's the thing to do. I wasn't a follow-the-leader type, but in front of my fellow GIs, I wanted to become a good soldier. They gave us the briefest course they could possibly give, and you hoped and prayed you'd never have to use this schooling because there was no way you had learned much, except to be frightened out of your wits. ★

Camp Croft, South Carolina - My Foray Into the Fruit Tart Business

When someone was assigned to KP, we had a standing agreement to bring back goodies for the barracks. If you happened to be fortunate enough to be assigned to the officers' mess, the rewards could be surprisingly good.

One day I was fortunate enough to be assigned to the officers' mess where the mess sergeant was preparing fruit tarts for dessert. I managed to sneak out four tarts and I took them back to the barracks. The guys liked them so much that they convinced me to get more. That afternoon, after our last meal, I stole 24 tarts. The dilemma was getting them out of the mess hall and back to the barracks.

> "I managed to sneak out four tarts and I took them back to the barracks. The guys liked them so much that they convinced me to get more."

I was setting up the mess tables for the following morning when I got this bright idea. For each place setting there was a cereal bowl turned face-down on a regular plate. I thought I was clever. I placed one tart under each bowl (24) for safekeeping until I could get them to the barracks. I felt very safe leaving the tarts there, so I went back to finish mopping the floors.

As luck would have it, the officer of the day pulled a surprise inspection in the mess hall. The sergeant called us all out and we had to stand at attention and wait for the officer and his aide to go through the hall. He came in with his white gloves, running his hands over furniture and the tables, and then he came to this one table and he turned over one of the bowls. I thought I'd die. But I had luck on my side because that was one of the tables where I *hadn't* hidden the tarts. As he went along I was keeping my fingers crossed and sweating bullets, just praying that he wouldn't turn over another bowl. He came up on the next table, turned over a bowl, and there sat a beautiful fruit tart. His eyes opened wide. His aide got a little smile on his face and my mess sergeant was as red as a beet. He was really pissed. The officer proceeded to turn over one bowl after another only to discover 24 freshly made tarts.

Of course, then they called in all of the mess boys. We all lined up and were threatened with a week of KP for everyone unless the one who did it owned up to it. So I very sheepishly stepped forward and admitted that I was the one who had put the tarts there. For my escapades I pulled three extra days of KP. I was given the dirtiest assignment in the kitchen for being a wiseass – cleaning the grease traps. Of course, the guys back in the barracks were disappointed that they didn't get their tarts.

The following day, the sergeant called me over and said, "Hey, Baby, how were you going to get those tarts out of there?" I showed him my ingenious plan. I would take paper napkins and wrap each tart. Then I would slide them down my pant leg. They wouldn't fall out because the ends of my pant legs were tucked into my leggings. He said, "You were going to walk all the way back to the barracks with them in there? You'd have had a mess." I told him, "Would you like me to show you?" He said, "Don't be such a smart-ass, I'll give you another three days' KP."

That was my foray into the fruit tart business. ★

Camp Croft – Traveling Steerage, Southern Style (Democracy at Its Best)

When I got my first pass and went into town, I took the local bus. I got on and took a seat. At the next stop a black girl got on. She was pregnant, and she had a baby in her arms. I got up to give her my seat. Her eyes opened wide and she was obviously shocked. The bus wasn't moving, and I told her to sit in my chair. The bus driver said, "Hey, white boy, sit down. And tell that nigger to get in the back." I said, "But she's pregnant." He said, "You sit down. This bus don't move until she goes back where she belongs, and you sit down where you belong or I'll throw you out." The girl got frightened and said, "No, sir, no sir. You sit!" and she went to the back.

"If this is supposed to be equality, someone had better read the Constitution."

I remember writing home and telling my family what a disgusting part of America I was in. If this is supposed to be equality, someone had better read the Constitution. I remember talking to some of the guys and we used to say, "How the hell can we say we're fighting for freedom when we still have this kind of prejudice and racial injustice?" ★

18

Camp Croft – Settling a Score

I remember one particularly terrible incident at Camp Croft in Spartanburg, South Carolina. Crosby, a typical redneck, thought he was a hot shit. On weekends he would go out and screw black girls. He used to pull out his penis and show off his warts, and brag that they "loved those French ticklers." I would ask him how he could brag about it, because he hated the blacks so much. How could he even touch them? He'd say, "I just fuck them." I detested him. I didn't consider him to be a man.

One afternoon when we were on a forced march we came upon a little black boy with a puppy. The puppy ran up to us, wiggling and wagging his tail. Suddenly Crosby swiped out with the butt of his rifle and crushed the puppy's head. As his eyes filled with tears, the little boy said, "What did you hurt him for? He didn't hurt nobody, he's my puppy." Crosby just laughed. I called Crosby a dirty sonofabitch. As the little boy was sobbing, Crosby just kept laughing.

We had a sergeant from Boston who knew that I hated Crosby's guts. He asked me, "You really want a piece of him, don't you?" I told the sergeant I'd love the opportunity to break Crosby's goddamned face. The sergeant warned me, "He's a lot bigger than you. He outweighs you by 30 pounds. I'd think about it before I started anything." I told him, "He may beat the shit out of me, but I'm going to break his nose." I knew I could do some damage to him. When I was a kid, 14 or 15 years old, I'd go to the Elks Club with my friends and warm up the fighters. They paid us $1.50 to use us like punching bags. (I remember one time they tried to pay us with kewpie dolls, like you'd get at a carnival. But we ganged up on the guy and made him pay cash.)

> "He may beat the shit out of me, but I'm going to break his nose."

19

Crosby was very good-looking and concerned about his face. I wanted to fix him good. The sergeant said, "How about this weekend before he gets his pass. I'll talk to some of the guys and they'll cover the windows so nobody can see in the barracks." When the weekend came, he told Crosby, "Before you get your pass, come over here. Baby wants to talk to you."

I called him a few names and he called me a nigger lover. He then said, "Crawby gonna cream you." But I wasn't afraid of him. I figured I could hold my own. They had moved all of the beds out of the way and we started fighting. He was giving me some good shots, jarring me pretty good, but I kept hanging in there. We fought all over the barracks. The other guys wouldn't let him wrestle me, they made him box. It was a good thing, too, because if he ever got hold of me, I'd be in trouble.

I kept going for Crosby's face because I knew if I broke his nose he'd stop, because he was so enamored of his looks. I finally got in the good shot I was waiting for, and his nose went "crunch." He grabbed his face and said, "Enough! Enough!" I called him every name under the sun and slapped him in the face but he wouldn't respond. Everybody was laughing at him except for some of his Southern buddies, but nobody really liked him.

When you have something in mind that you want to do and you know you're right, your determination and conviction can sometimes bring you Herculean strength. It's unbelievable. When he hit me it was almost like I didn't feel the blows because I was determined to break his nose and get revenge for that little boy. ★

Camp Croft – The City Boy Becomes a Kentucky Sharpshooter

My first experience with a rifle was a .22 caliber. This was the Army way of getting us acclimated to firearms. Much to my surprise, I was quite good. Going through all the drills I consistently hit the bull's-eye and my permanent cadre was elated. At the time I was not aware that each sergeant was assigned a scout to teach. They would bet against each other for quite a bit of money on who had the best rifleman. My sergeant was so excited, he thought he had a sure winner. I found out he was betting pretty heavily on our squad. But this guy was an SOB and I decided to teach him a lesson.

When we got to the rifle range with our M1s, I could hear him talking about the bets and he was just waiting for me to get up on the firing line. There were some pretty good shooters. (That's when I first found out about "Maggie's drawers." They had spotters, and if you missed completely, they would wave Maggie's drawers.) When it came my turn to lie down in a prone position, I sighted the target and my first shot went right in. He got excited and I decided now was my chance to get even with the SOB. I shot my full clip and all I got was Maggie's drawers. He cursed and cursed. When we had a second round, he threatened me and I said, "I'll do better, Sarge." And I repeated my performance. Just to piss him off, I put the first one in the bull's-eye and for the rest I played around with Maggie's drawers. I wanted to be sure that he was going to lose his bet.

When I got off the range he called me over and said, "You little SOB. I know exactly what you did. You'll pay for this." Every day he made me run an extra obstacle course under the southern sun. At one session when he made me run and I kept smiling, he said, "I'll wipe that smile off your face." On the course, I had to dash about 100 yards and leap a pit. Then there was a series of low fences to vault and another 100 yards to run, weaving in and out of obstacles. After the obstacles I had to vault another fence and run

25 yards to a 10 foot wall that I had to scamper up and dive over. He worked me over. I was a pretty good athlete and I could run. Finally, I succumbed to heat exhaustion and instead of leaping over the wall, I fell off. One of the corporals said he'd carried it too far. They put me in the hospital for observation and then he decided to lay off me. ★

Camp Croft – Basic Training Simulated Battle Conditions

Land Mines, Barbed Wire, and Booby Traps

In basic training there was a pattern of putting the recruits through the roughest drills before we had a meal. So at the end of one day, we were informed that the following morning we would go through a machine gun fire and booby trap course. The next day, before breakfast, we reported to the course and were lined up in twos. An instructor demonstrated how to crawl under strands of barbed wire. At the end of the field they had set up two .30 caliber, water-cooled machine guns, one on the left and the other on the right. The guns were set to fire live ammunition 36" above the ground, creating crossfire. The effect was as close to a battlefield experience as possible. The atmosphere was tense and pretty scary. We were warned under no circumstances to jump up or raise our heads, and to hug the ground as closely as possible. There were small dirt mounds scattered around, set with booby

traps that would explode, sometimes close to your face. In my case, when I started to crawl and got under the first set of barbed wires, there was an explosion near me. I jerked my head down. Later on, when I com-

pleted the course, they discovered a crack in my helmet.

Sometimes you started off crawling on your belly, but usually as you approached the wires, the easiest way was to turn over on your back, push the barbed wire up with your weapon, and snake your way underneath. While we were crawling under the wire it seemed forever, that you would never get to the other side. The machine guns chattered away

23

the whole time. Sometimes they would set off the traps even if you didn't run into them, so that you would get accustomed to the conditions of war. It was scary because it was the first time I had encountered live ammunition. Unfortunately, during this exercise one of the guys panicked. He jerked his body up to avoid an explosion, and he was hit in the shoulder.

We learned later that one of the previous recruits had been killed. I don't know if it was a story to make us remember to keep our heads down, or if it was the truth, but one of our guys did get shot in the arm and I had a cracked helmet.

Learning to Throw Live Grenades

Another skill we needed to master was throwing live grenades. They told us that once we pulled the pin and released the trigger arm, we only had so many seconds before a grenade would explode. I remember the first one I threw. In my anxiety, I forgot to pull out the pin. We all got a big laugh out of that episode, but I got pretty good at the grenade business. Metal stovepipes were set into the dirt to simulate mortars, and I threw a grenade in the top of one and blew it up. I was the hero for that.

Classroom Training

In the classroom we learned to identify all enemy planes, both German and Japanese. Pictures and silhouettes of planes would flash on a screen and we soon could identify them by their shape. We needed to be very sure during this drill. When we got into combat, a mistake could be deadly. At a certain angle, our American Corsairs, even though they had gull wings, almost looked like a Japanese Zero.

We practiced communicating with brief messages to describe situations when we were scouting. The messages had to be brief but contain all the critical information. We learned to operate walkie-talkies and radios and to observe with binoculars. The binoculars had grids so we could estimate distance. We learned to study terrain and use our judgment to determine where the Japanese would have fortifications or set up weapons. We had plenty of chances to apply our classroom training in the field.

House to House (Street Fighting)

We were marched off to an actual village that had been set up, complete with houses and stores. As we approached the site, the sergeant ordered us to get on our bellies and two of us were assigned the duty of scout. Little did I know then that I'd soon actually be a scout in combat. The scouts were to reconnoiter the area for enemy locations and report back to the squad leader if it was clear for us to move into the area.

Our squad was split in half, each group patrolling one side of the street. We went from house to house. The houses were built to simulate a real village, so we actually climbed through a window or pushed open a door to get in. We were trained to cover each other. As you moved in, suddenly a silhouette of an enemy soldier would pop up. They would "fire" at us. If you heard that noise, you were dead or wounded. If you could hit the silhouette before it fired at you, it was rigged to disengage. It was as realistic as you could possibly get.

Rope suspension bridges swung when you tried to cross them. There were streams where we had to swing across the water on ropes. Dense foliage hid the enemy, simulating jungle warfare. That gave us a little taste of the Pacific. There was also a separate area with shops and houses in a European setting. There we fought from house to house. We did this for several days, and each time we went through one of the exercises we had to write a report on what we saw. We wrote brief notes on very small memo paper. Along with our classroom instruction, this was our introduction to intelligence and reconnaissance.

The Gas Chamber

In the Army one was trained to cope with the unexpected. At reveille one morning, our sergeant read the order of the day – the gas chambers. Before breakfast we were issued gas masks. To make sure that no skin was exposed to the gas, we were required to wear full uniform. Of course, the GIs had a wonderful time joking about our private gas chambers (our sleeping quarters). One wise guy with a great sense of humor said, "How bad can it be? Eating Army food puts us through a gas attack every night!"

My father had served in World War I. The one experience that stood out the most in his mind was the gas attacks in the battle at the Verdun Front. I remember the feeling of horror when he described the soldiers in the trenches — the cries of pain and the difficulty breathing when the shells with the canisters of gas would fall among the soldiers. He especially remembered the Scottish infantry (they were called the ladies from hell). They wore kilts, so they were vulnerable to the ravages of mustard gas. He said the poor bastards were burned by the mustard gas over their body, including their private parts. Mustard gas will contaminate your clothes and cause burns and blistering, long after exposure. This picture always stuck in my mind.

That morning we were called out and lined up in front of two Quonset huts. One hut was the mustard gas chamber and the other contained phosgene gas. We were strongly cautioned not to touch our eyes after we left the hut, until we had washed, because we would be contaminated by the gas.

First we entered the phosgene hut. We started with our gas masks on, and the drill was to take them off for a few seconds and then put them back on. In battle, we would need to handle situations like this without panicking. Some of the guys did panic, and had to be taken out. Some even threw up.

26

We dealt with the phosgene gas for a short time, then we entered the mustard gas hut. Again, a couple of the guys started throwing up, and a couple had to be carried out because they panicked and passed out. When we emerged from the hut, we took off our masks and we were ordered to go back to the barracks to shower and change our clothes. We had to make sure not to touch any of the contaminated material and then touch ourselves.

Finally, we got to go to breakfast, but many of us were sick to our stomachs and we had no appetite. ★

Camp Croft – A Yankee Gets His Comeuppance at the USO

On a weekend pass I went over to Greensboro to an Army canteen dance with four of my buddies. The Southern belles were the hostesses. The event took place in a building like a church hall. It was decorated with crepe paper streamers for the occasion and they had punch and homemade baked goods and cookies for the GIs. The hostess was very gracious and showed no sign of prejudice. She welcomed us warmly and told us to enjoy ourselves.

> *"I don't dance with no Yankees."*

There was a band playing '40s music — "I'm Getting Tired So I Can Sleep, I Want to Sleep So I Can Dream of You," "Missed the Saturday Dance," "The Jersey Bounce," "I'll Never Smile Again," "Every Night About This Time, Oh, How I Miss You,"… and an Artie Shaw tune, "Begin the Beguine." The guys were excited to be meeting girls. We were awestruck. The girls wore very pretty summer dresses, and they looked fresh and beautiful.

My friend Moe Cohen said to me, "Davinko, I think that girl is sizing you up. I think she really likes you!" The guys kept pushing me to go over and talk to her. I was a little shy, so I held off for a long time, but they kept egging me on. Finally, they convinced me that I should ask her to dance. She had some pretty girlfriends, and of course they wanted to be introduced.

So I walked over and introduced myself and asked the girl if she'd like to dance. She sure set me straight. She proceeded to tell me, "I don't dance with no *Yankees*." My wide-eyed image of them was shattered. I looked at Moe as if to say, "Look what you got me into!" Moe answered, "You win some and lose some."

So my first attempt at the social graces below the Mason-Dixon Line blew up right in my face. ★

Camp Croft – My Friend, Moe Cohen

My friend Moe Cohen was in communications. As part of his training he had to learn to string wire. It involved climbing poles just like any telephone or electrical worker would do. You strap spikes on your legs and have a belt on your waist. You have to learn to trust yourself by leaning back and climbing up. Moe did just fine climbing up. But on the way down, instead of leaning back and releasing some slack, he pulled himself in close to the pole and broke the record for coming down. He skinned his legs and was a total mess when he hit the ground.

Pfc. Moe Cohen

Moe had a reputation for playing the game and getting away without doing much. He used the excuse, "I don't know how," like a child whose mother tells him to do something he doesn't want to do. He had a lazy approach to things that he didn't consider important.

Moe's philosophy was that there were enough people out there ready to kill him, so he wasn't going to kill himself. But when it counted, Moe was a real soldier and a good soldier.

As fate would have it, some of the guys who mistreated Moe came overseas later on after Moe and I were already seasoned veterans. Moe, instead of taking revenge on them, was kind enough to forget the past and deal with them as poor bastards who had to fight a war just like the rest of us. ★

Fort Meade – The Wrong Way – The Right Way – The Army Way

After Camp Croft we went to Fort Meade, a staging area for overseas duty. We were issued winter clothes, and everyone thought we were going to the European theater. I was excited because I spoke Italian and it made sense that I could be useful in Europe. But after a few days for processing at Fort Meade, the Army screwed up and we were sent to Shalmoth's Slip, New Orleans, a shipping out point for the Pacific. At Shalmoth's Slip they took back our winter clothes and reissued hot weather gear. Typical military. I suppose there was some reason for all of this, but in 60-odd years I haven't figured out how the military thinks.

By the way, Fort Meade was a prostitute's paradise. The houses of prostitution were off-limits for us. We were issued "pro kits" for protection from disease. If we didn't use the kit and we caught a disease, we could be court-martialed and dishonorably discharged. They showed us movies that scared the crap out of us. We were there a short time, and they did give us leave to go into town and relax before we shipped out. Half of the young recruits never left the camp, me included.

There were girls who were not prostitutes, who were very willing to meet the troops. Some young ladies would frequent a certain area where they could meet soldiers. They were called "security girls" and the soldiers were allowed to date them. It was explained to me that most of the security girls were clean, very nice, very pretty, and very determined to get married. They married the soldiers for their insurance. They would get $10,000 if their husband didn't come back from the war. The presence of security girls was so common that the drill sergeants had a little ditty about them to keep cadence when we marched. "Security broads will get you in bed…They marry you, then they wish you're dead!…"

"Laundry girls" made a living washing and ironing our clothes. There were no laundry facilities for us to use, so they had quite a good business. We'd hire them to do our laundry and when we got the clothes back, we'd find notes in our pockets with the name and address and phone number of the laundry girl. They were interested in marriage, too, but not necessarily for romance. They, too, wanted to collect the insurance if their GI husband was killed in the war. One girl was arrested for multiple marriages. She had collected $30,000 by marrying three different guys and all three happened to get killed. The whole business seemed ghoulish. ★

Shalmoth's Slip, New Orleans, Louisiana - Frenchy for a Dollar

We were scheduled to go to the Pacific by way of the Panama Canal. One night, my friend Moe Cohen got the idea that since we only had a few days before they shipped us out, we should go see New Orleans. Some of the guys said there was a place where you could break out of the compound. Moe thought maybe we could pick up some girls. We got out, boarded a bus, and managed to get to the French Quarter. There was a red light district there and Moe started talking to some of the girls. I hung back because I had never even been out on a date. Moe met this mulatto girl and she said, "You come on, I'll show you Frenchy for two dollars." I told Moe I didn't want to go. He asked me why not. We had been seeing movies about VD and how awful it was. I told him, "No, I don't want to go. You never know what you're going to pick up." Moe thought about it and decided I was right. We walked away from her. She chased us, calling, "You SOBs come 'ere! I gonna show you Frenchy for two dollars!" Then she said, "I'll show you Frenchy for a dollar!" I asked Moe, "Who's Frenchy?" And Moe said, "Give her a dollar and she'll show you who Frenchy is!" We took off running like scared rabbits. We were 18. What the hell did we know. That was our adventure in New Orleans. ★

> "You come on, I'll show you Frenchy for two dollars."

Shalmoth's Slip, Louisiana – Shipping Out

In camp during the day we trained, practicing with bayonets. This asshole from Texas who used to call me "Mac-i-ninni" was assigned as my partner for training. He was supposed to thrust, I would block it, and he would give me a vertical stroke with the butt of his rifle. It was to be a simulated stroke, with no actual contact. But this SOB bashed me right in the nose. I went down on my knees. I tried to get up, I wanted to kill the bastard. But I was hurting too bad. I just kept stumbling, trying to catch him. He kept trying to apologize. They took me to the aid station, where they just put two sticks up my nose with cotton to stop the bleeding, and taped it. We were leaving the next day and they didn't want to hospitalize me, so they said I'd be fine. The next day we got on trucks to be transported to the ship. We were going to embark for the Pacific.

I had never been on an ocean ship. It was a cruise ship that had been converted to a troop carrier. You felt like you were on a slave ship. Once on board, we went down into the hold where we slept in tiers of bunks. I was unlucky enough to draw the top tier. I was so close to the ceiling and it was so hot that I felt like I was suffocating. It was terrible.

We were given instructions on how to put on our life vests, and assigned life stations. When we got far into the Gulf of Mexico heading down toward the Panama Canal, an alarm went off and we had to go on deck and put on our gear. I later learned that German submarines were lurking about, watching for ships. As a result, we were escorted by corvette sub chasers that would drop depth charges all around us. I'll never forget the sound of the corvettes. They had sirens that wailed. They kept cutting in and out, back and forth in our path. They were like hornets buzzing around, trying to find the subs. We didn't know if they sank any subs, but we managed to get safely down to the Panama Canal with our convoy.

I remember going through the locks, and other soldiers and civilians waving to us as we sailed by. We got to the other side and thought we were going to have an escort to the Pacific, but we were sent out without an escort. We were to sail between protective lanes, although I never knew who was protecting the lanes because we never saw any war ships on either side of us.

On the ship there wasn't much to do so the guys would gamble, and some of the pots got really big. They talked me into gambling with them. I had a few dollars on me, and with beginner's luck, I won $700, more money than I'd ever seen! They tried to get me back into the game to get their money back, but I wouldn't do it. I told them, "I'm not a gambler. I don't gamble." I took the money and I couldn't wait to wire it home to my family. ★

Bora Bora – The Jewel of the Pacific

We had an uneventful voyage to British New Guinea, but we did have a very interesting one-day stopover at the Island of Bora Bora, the jewel of the Pacific. We had to take on supplies and fuel.

As we approached one of the inlets of Bora Bora, the water in the bay was crystal clear. It seemed like you could see down a hundred feet. From the shore, dozens of canoes and dugouts came out to greet us. Our hosts threw leis and flowers all around the ship. They were like children – beautiful young men and beautiful girls. We threw coins in the water and they would dive for them. It was like a scene from a tropical movie.

We traded our change for trinkets and fruit. I love bananas, so I bought a bunch of them. They were green, and I figured they would last for the rest of the trip. Unfortunately, I found out that they were for cooking.

One of the guys on board saw me sketching, and he offered me watercolor paints that he'd brought with him. I was so grateful. I wanted to capture the spirit of Bora Bora as best I could, to send to my family. Of course, my mother saved the painting and it still brings back memories of that island paradise. ★

Watercolor painting of Bora Bora by Dave Mancini

British New Guinea – Man's Inhumanity to Man

It took us about 28 days to travel from Shalmoth's Slip to British New Guinea. When we finally arrived and walked down the ramp, there were GIs around who were with the 19th Infantry. We were joining their unit. They had been stationed in Oahu, and the outfit was made up of regulars and ex-criminals who, if their offenses weren't too bad, were given a choice of either joining up or staying in jail. Unbeknownst to us young ones, they were sizing us up as we came down the ramp. They were lecherous bastards. They were accustomed to visiting the whorehouse in Oahu. They hadn't had a girl in so long that we looked good to them. We were still kids. Many of us didn't shave and had smooth, hairless skin.

There was a Sergeant Bumgardner who took a particular liking to me and gave me candy bars. He told me, "Stick with me, kid, and I'll show you the ropes around here." He was soliciting me. Thank God, I was befriended by a young medic from Kansas. He was about 28 years old. We used to call him Doc. He called me aside and said, "Don't pay attention to him. Be careful because he's looking for a boy. Do you understand what I'm trying to tell you?" I had written a letter home telling my family how helpful the older soldiers were and how nice they were treating me. But when Doc warned me about what this guy was after, I told Bumgardner to stay away. I ignored him and tried to stay away from him. I actually slept with my rifle.

One day, we were showering under these 90-gallon drums. They put holes in the bottoms of the drums and made a shower. The guys would have someone soap their backs or wash it for them. Bumgardner came behind me and said, "Wash my back, kid." So I took the soap and washed it and he said he'd wash mine. I hesitated, and soon I realized he was breathing heavily and making strange noises while he was rubbing my back. I wheeled around and saw that he had an erection and was masturbating. I punched him right in the face. I caught him by surprise and warned him to stay the fuck away from me. I told him, "If you ever come near me again, I'll put a bullet in your head!" He gave me a big smile and said, "I'll get even with you, Baby." And he did, in his own way. He found out that I had boxed a little when I was younger. Every now and then we would set up some entertainment for the troops. I weighed 139 and he weighed 180. They set up a schedule and I was to box him. I gave him as much as I could, but he was too strong and he was a seasoned fighter. He made sure he beat the shit out of me.

Most of us were smart enough to stay away from these lecherous bastards, but there was one guy who was a farm seed and he wanted to be one of the boys. He was a big kid, over six feet tall. He was sort of round and overweight and had white skin and rosy cheeks. The older guys kept trying to get him in their group.

One night the older soldiers decided to have a big party. We told the farm boy not to go but he said we were crazy and they wouldn't do anything to him. They kept feeding him homemade "jungle juice" and got him drunk. They forced him over a fallen coconut tree, pulled down his pants, and lined up on him. A couple of the sergeants tried to break it up, but they said, "If you come over here, we'll kill you." They had all been drinking, and by the time they got the officers there, they had already done a job on this kid. There were at least ten or more of them and they cheered each other on like animals. Some even came back for seconds. The next day when he woke up, the kid discovered that his bottom was bleeding and realized what had happened. They were all kidding and laughing and telling him what a great lay he was. He went out of his mind and tried to kill himself. They had to send him back to the States.

As young soldiers, we discovered the meaning of "man's inhumanity to man," and we hadn't even seen any combat yet. ★

British New Guinea – My First Combat Assignment, Guard Duty

On my first night in British New Guinea, right after we landed six of us were assigned to guard an ammunition depot. The corporal of the guards took us out and dropped us off at our designated post. I was 18 years old. It was pitch black and all I could hear were jungle noises, and I was scared shitless. (Later on, I found out that all six of us who were so gung ho and hadn't even encountered the enemy yet, were ready to shit our pants.) The ammunition was in stacks and surrounded with barbed wire. It was dark and we were scared because we were told that even though the Japanese army on New Guinea was defeated, there were still stragglers left. Every now and then they would come in on a suicide mission and try to blow up some heavy artillery, especially ammunition dumps. Although the Australians had driven most of them up into the hills, we still had to take precautions.

That night as I was walking my post, I heard what sounded like the heavy wing movement of a very large bird. It seemed as though there were hundreds of them. In the dark, my imagination ran wild. Looking up, I saw what appeared to be enormous, prehistoric birds and they were making squeaking sounds. My courage just ran out of me like a stream of urine. I worked my way in between some of the ammunition boxes and hid. I managed to peek at my watch to check when my two-hour shift was up, so I would be walking my post when the corporal came with my relief.

Standing guard in New Guinea ammunition dump

When I came back to camp, I asked the guys what those huge birds were that were flying around. Some of the older vets laughed and told me they were bats. One of them said, "It's a wonder you didn't shoot one. On my first day, I shot at one and got the whole camp in an uproar. You can do two things. You either shoot or be blind to what's out there."

As time passed and I got accustomed to the war, I was never as frightened as I was that first night in the pitch dark jungle with the bats. ★

Dutch New Guinea – Typhoon

Going to the first invasion of Dutch New Guinea, the waves were so high that the bow of the ship would submerge. I pulled two duties – four hours on the forward gun, strapped in so that I wouldn't be washed overboard. I was there because Army personnel were utilized to relieve the sailors. I was soaking wet, and when I saw sailors getting sick, I got sick. For 24 hours I just kept throwing up. My stomach was empty, and then with the dry heaves, I was in pain but at the same time I was as hungry as a bear.

I spotted this can in the galley and I grabbed it and ran downstairs below deck in my bunk. When I opened it, I found figs in heavy syrup. I started eating them and passing them around. But then the mess officers discovered their count was off, and they were looking for the can.

I gave myself away when I had to report a bad case of diarrhea. ★

Dutch New Guinea – Old People

Because we ran into a typhoon on the way to Dutch New Guinea, they called off the invasion and we landed on another part of the island that was under Australian control. The invasion was merely postponed and would proceed in a couple of weeks when the weather was more favorable.

While I was on one of the islands, I discovered a place where the natives put their old people to die. I was ordered to scout around, and proceeded along the beach. Eventually I came upon very old people who could barely move or talk. They had been sent there by their families. They were too old to do anything useful, so they were put there to die. They had little lean-tos set up. If they didn't get food, they starved. Some of them just lay there with their mouths open and flies crawling on them. I was shocked that this was part of New Guinea's native culture. ★

Dutch New Guinea – Fear Is Deadly
April 22, 1944

On the way to the invasion of Dutch New Guinea, one kid jumped off the ship. They thought he fell overboard. One of our escort ships picked him up. He was so scared, he jumped off again. They forced him to be one of the first out of the landing craft and he was so frightened that he went berserk. They had to tie him up and bring him back to the ship. We never saw him again. ★

Dutch New Guinea – Marcelino Delgado

I met Marcelino Delgado in the invasion of New Guinea. The Japanese had put up very little resistance and had retreated to the hills. We were stationed near the Hollandia airstrip. There were two of us scouting the airstrip when we discovered a Japanese supply dump. However, we were caught in crossfire by some Jap stragglers. This BAR* man came out from behind one of the buildings and gave the Japs a couple of bursts. He killed one and the others took off. We introduced ourselves, and that's when Marcelino and I became very good friends.

Marcelino was an entrepreneur. Being a very resourceful guy, when he discovered that I was an artist, he figured out a way to make some money. He asked me if I knew how to engrave. I told him that if I had the tools, I could. So he took the firing pin from a BAR and sharpened it down to a fine point so I could cut into metal. Being on an airstrip, we had shot up quite a few Japanese Zeros and other planes, and the metal was light enough that Marcelino could make it into bracelets. I made templates for him and traced them, and he would cut out wristbands. I would engrave them "With Love" for special days like Mother's Day, and the soldiers would send them home to their mothers. There came a point when we dove for cat-eyes and we soldered them onto the bracelets, and I would engrave around them. He said all I had to do was the artwork and he would do the rest. He took charge of selling them because, as he said, "Keed, you're a bad businessman."

We managed to split $500 one time, and $700 another. Around Valentine's Day I was turning out dozens of bracelets. Marcelino and I developed quite a friendship through our business. During our entrepreneurial endeavor, I learned that he was a pimp back in the States. He still had three prostitutes working for him while he was away. His English wasn't very good so I would read the letters they sent to him and would write letters back for him. We developed a very deep friendship over time.

When I was wounded, he somehow followed my trail and discovered that I was in Halloran General Hospital on Staten Island. One day, while I was lying in bed, someone said I had some visitors. In walked these three gorgeous girls. They said Marcelino had sent them. They brought me cards and flowers and for two months they came to see me every week. I had a note from him in Spanish which they translated for me. In the letter he said that when he came back to the States, he would show me the best time I had ever had in my life. All the guys in my ward were envious of me but I think they all suspected that the girls were hookers.

> "During our entrepreneurial endeavor, I learned he was a pimp back in the States."

I'm sorry to say that I never heard from him. The girls stopped coming by and I have always wondered if he was killed, or what happened to him. This "Keed" is really sorry that he lost touch with his friend Marcelino. ★

Browning automatic rifle - light machine gun that looked like and was carried like a large rifle with a tripod.

Marcelino Delgado

Dutch New Guinea – Superman

I remember an incident on my first scouting mission in New Guinea. Having been assigned to Intelligence and Reconnaissance, the Army had tried to simulate combat situations as closely as possible, but there's nothing like the real thing. I was taken out with two other new recruits to be trained by a sergeant and three veteran soldiers. We were deployed as a group of seven to gather information as a scouting group and to try to capture prisoners, too. We were cautioned to be very quiet. This was a real mission and I was scared to death. We were all very frightened, but there was a calmness about the experienced soldiers that helped to relieve some of our fear. At the time I felt we were relatively secure.

But as we were going up a hill, one recruit got so nervous that a grenade fell from his belt and he hollered, "Grenade!" We all hit the ground, waiting for the worst. He sheepishly said, "It was *my* grenade." The grenade had just dropped. A grenade doesn't explode unless you pull the pin. The sergeant wanted to kill him since the Japanese had now been alerted that we were in the area. We very cautiously moved down the trail and up an incline. It was almost a dead silence. Then we began to hear bird whistles all around us. They sounded like a typical bird you would hear in the jungle, but there were too many of

Dave Mancini, left, in Dutch New Guinea - 1944

them. Animals don't usually stir or make noise while humans

43

are around and it seemed strange to hear birds chirping. The sergeant, who was very familiar with these sounds, told us to be quiet as the enemy was near. As we came up over a ridge, gunfire suddenly opened up. The Japanese had surrounded us on three sides.

We were lucky. On our right were fallen logs. We hit the ground and the logs provided us with some cover. But this being my first mission, I was facing the wrong way. I was facing open ground. The sergeant grabbed me by my cartridge belt and lifted me off the ground. He said, "What the hell are you shooting at? On this side!" He kept me near him. He would tap each one of us and tell us to go over a bank on the right where there was no enemy fire. As he tapped each one, they would go over the logs and down the hill. That was the only escape route. As the sergeant tapped each soldier, I noticed they very cautiously crawled over the logs. I couldn't understand why they didn't just jump right over. I was one of the last ones to go and when the sergeant tapped me on the shoulder and said, "Go!," I dove over the logs.

"What the hell are you shooting at?"

Unbeknownst to me, we were on the edge of a cliff. I went flying in the air over the tops of trees. Luckily, those trees broke my fall and saved my life. I lost my helmet and gear, but of course I was the first one down the cliff. Everyone was laughing because we had escaped and for a while they called me "Superman." Although we were nearly cornered, my acrobatics broke the stress of a very dangerous situation. ★

Dutch New Guinea –
Hollandia Airfield *(Japanese Air Base)*

On my second mission they sent me out with a veteran. We were looking for Japanese near one of their airstrips, the Hollandia Airfield. We knew the Japanese had established a command post in the area. Shortly after we set out, we spotted some Japanese communication wire and we started to follow it. After very carefully picking our way, we discovered an observation and communication hut that the Japanese had built. It was also a pilot or officers' quarters. As I kicked in the door, I was confronted by a Japanese soldier about 15 feet away from me. A knife came at me, Wham! I ducked. I had my rifle trained on him but I froze because I had never killed a man before. Suddenly a deafening shot rang out behind me and the Japanese soldier dropped to the floor. The veteran scout had saved my life. He told me that if I wanted to live, I'd better learn to pull the trigger. Close my eyes if I had to, but "pull the goddamned trigger." If I didn't, I wouldn't last very long. It turned out the Japanese soldier was with the Imperial Marines. He'd been wounded and left behind.

I had seen dead bodies on the beach and bodies that were bloated from the sun as we pushed from the New Guinea beaches to Hollandia airstrip. I felt sadness and remorse, but in my nervousness and a feeling for self-preservation, I tried to ignore the dead bodies. But when I saw a man killed a few feet in front of me, that was my first realization that war was even worse than I had imagined. This wasn't a movie set, this was real and the deaths were real. Not like some John Wayne bullshit. ★

Dutch New Guinea – Surprises at Hollandia

When we captured Hollandia airstrip, we had a few unexpected surprises. The Japanese pilots were supplied with sake, which we discovered in the supplies that they had left behind when we drove them out. Of course, the American troops were all too ready to celebrate their victory.

We went tracking through the jungle and the guys were drunk all the way. If there had been a Japanese force nearby, our guys would have been sitting ducks. The officers also found these little confetti candies. But instead of being filled with an almond, they were filled with dope – except nobody knew it. The guys helped themselves, thinking it was ordinary candy, and discovered afterwards that they were groggy. I even had one and did not realize what I had gotten into until I felt a buzz.

During this period we were on patrol and we captured a Japanese soldier. We dragged him into the compound and one of our Southern redneck SOBs wanted to see him commit hara-kiri. They formed a circle around him and threw in a knife, but a sergeant stepped in and broke it up.

In the meantime, another Japanese prisoner broke away. One of the guys wrestled him to the ground and discovered in the scuffle that it was a woman. In the early part of the war it was not uncommon that geisha girls were provided to the Japanese officers, especially for those in the air corps. She was, in fact, a geisha for the Japanese officers. The interpreter told us that she was afraid she would be raped if it was discovered that she was a woman, so she dressed in one of the pilot's uniforms. We turned her over to the MPs and medics. That was the last we saw of her. ★

Dutch New Guinea –
Defending My Sister's Honor

While in New Guinea I met a rough-and-tumble group of men who were called Pioneers. They were a team of six men originally from the Pennsylvania coal mining district. The majority of them were of Slavic origin. One of them, the sergeant in charge, was at least 6'4" and easily 230-240 pounds. There wasn't an inch of fat on him. They were friendly with everyone, but all of the young recruits and many of the old-timers were a little bit leery of the Pioneers and stayed clear of them. They were experts at handling explosives because of their experience in the mines, and their main job was to build bridges and then take them down with explosives. My curiosity got the best of me and I sort of liked their rough-

21 year old Clara Mancini - 1943

and-tumble ways. I liked to listen to them talk and I was lucky at times to sit at their table when we had chow.

One day after mail call, I opened a letter from home. It was my sister's 21st birthday and she had sent me a picture of herself. I was so proud of her because she was so beautiful and such a nice person. One of the guys grabbed the picture from me. They asked me if it was my girlfriend, and they were raving about her beauty and passing the picture around. The picture finally reached the sergeant and he made some admiring remarks but then said, "I'll bet she's a great piece of ass!" I instinctively threw a hot cup of coffee in his face. I flew over the table, all 138 pounds of me, and hit him as hard as I could.

47

The sergeant fell backwards, not from my blows but from the hot coffee, and he ended up on his back with me on top of him throwing the best punches I could possibly muster from my flimsy arms. I probably felt like a fly to him. From a prone position he lifted me up, held me in midair, struggled to his feet, walked me to a tree, and bashed me against it three times. It rattled every bone in my body. My head was spinning. He pulled me close to him and said, "You little shit, if I didn't like you, I'd break every bone in your body right now!" He put me down and glared at me.

> *"You little shit, if I didn't like you, I'd break every bone in your body."*

Then he said to the bystanders, "Don't you ever laugh at this kid. He's got more guts than all of you. He had guts enough to confront me. Not one of you would have spoken up to challenge me. I've got your number!" They all kept quiet. After that he would always invite me to sit at their table and I became his friend. He even taught me to blow up a tree with explosive putty. He was like my protector until the time we parted. ★

Dutch New Guinea – Recreation

While we were unloading ships, part of our recreation on a rest day was to swim out to the large LSTs* and dive off the front ramp. They were anchored way out in the harbor in very deep water. I couldn't swim, so I would sit in envy watching as the other guys swam out there. After watching everyone else having fun, I couldn't stand it any longer. We had these small flotation pillows that we used to help us cross streams and deep water. I grabbed a couple, stuffed one up under my shirt, and paddled my way out to the LSTs even though I couldn't swim a stroke. I could always dive and come up and get back to the ramp, but I couldn't go any real distance.

> "Once you've been in combat, you don't feel fear of anything."

In retrospect, it was a crazy thing to be doing. But once you've been in combat, you don't feel fear of anything. You almost feel invincible. If those pillows ever deflated, there was no way I could get back to shore. ★

*Landing Ship Transport

Dutch New Guinea – Broken Hearts — Live While You Can

As we moved north of Hollandia after occupying the airstrip, we met pockets of resistance. Although the Japanese were on the run and scattered, it was very difficult for us to finish our mopping up operation because they still managed to entrench themselves in some areas. Routinely, we were ordered to go out in rotation and scout around to see if we could identify any situation that called for an air strike. There was one particular area where the Japanese had a big gun. They had it well camouflaged in heavy jungle foliage at the base of one of the mountains. It was playing hell with some of our troops. So on this day, three of us were sent out with a radio so we could call back if we needed some firepower.

After proceeding a short distance, we heard a large gun but we couldn't see it. We reached a hill that was situated so that we could walk around the side of it to the front, and look down and observe the whole valley. We were taking turns using the field glasses, so many minutes off and on, so our eyes wouldn't get tired. After about the third pass, I spotted some movement. I watched the Japanese pull back this camouflage netting and out would peek this big gun that maneuvered in and out so fast it must have been mounted on something like a railroad track. It would fire, pull back, and the camouflage would drop down. In my excitement, I jumped up. I don't know if I exposed myself or not, but somehow they knew we were there. When I came around the hill to tell the other scouts, one of them ran around to look with his field glasses. While I was explaining to the radio man what to radio back, a shell came in and slammed right into the side of the mountain where we were. I was knocked off my feet. The radio man got hit pretty badly, but we knew the guy up front was more seriously hurt. We could hear him crying. I crawled out and helped him back. I held him as he cried. He kept calling out for his mother. He died in my arms.

The other scout was hurt, but I was very fortunate. My ear and nose were bleeding and my ears were ringing from the concussion of the shell, but I was still coherent enough to radio back the position. Shortly after we called back and gave the coordinates, a 105 half-track came up and blasted right where the Japanese position was.

I can't recall the name of the soldier who died, but the one who was sent off to the hospital was "Jim." I was field treated for the ringing in my ears and headache. I had a gouge in my ankle and a little sliver of metal in my back, a fragment of something. It was a surface wound, so they pulled it out and just bandaged me up. I suppose I was entitled to a Purple Heart for my wounds, but at the time that was not something that even occurred to me. It certainly wasn't important.

I think the saddest thing that came to my mind was that here we were, three teenagers but still grown men, and I can remember the one who was wounded so badly calling for his mother. It seemed when the end was so close, and being the age we were, we hadn't been weaned yet to be far from our parents, so we still called out to them and clung to them for comfort.

"Don't get too close to anyone. You don't want to attach yourself to anybody too closely. All you do is keep losing them."

The next day I was sent out with the instrument corporal. He was setting up machine guns and I went with him to try to point out where some of the Japanese positions were. They started to set up machine gun nests overlooking the valley the Japanese would have to traverse if they attacked us. I remember the instrument corporal telling me,

"Don't get too close to anyone." His name was Corporal Kissling. "You don't want to attach yourself closely to any-body, because all you do is lose them." There were too many disappointments and too many broken hearts over attach-ments. Some of the guys used to say, "Here today, gone tomorrow. Live while you can." ★

Dutch New Guinea –
Meeting the "Fuzzy-Wuzzies"

After the Dutch New Guinea campaign, the 24th Division was regrouping in a rest area. A buddy of mine named Dick, from Buffalo, New York, suggested that we venture out and scout around the island. He thought maybe we could trade with some of the native tribes for souvenirs. Some veterans who overheard us talking warned us that we weren't seasoned enough to understand what was going on around us. They told us to be careful and warned us not to wander too deep into the jungle, because there were head-hunters.

Because I was in Intelligence and Reconnaissance, I had some maps. We figured we could find our way. We had our weapons and weren't too concerned. We decided to risk it, and set out up a hill into the jungle. After about an hour of trekking we heard some rustling and realized we were very close to a village. We decided to walk in and see what was going on. When we got there, we saw huts, but it was very quiet and there weren't any people around. There weren't even any dogs barking. It was eerie and it made my skin crawl. I thought maybe there had been a disaster of some kind, or the Japs had forced the villagers away. In the center of the compound stood a half-hut. A picture of Queen Wilhelmina of Holland hung on a pole in the middle. Because this was Dutch New Guinea, the natives revered her as their authority figure.

After a short time, the villagers began to appear. They wore nothing but little loincloths that hung in the front. They carried hardened wooden spears and bows and arrows, and began circling around us. We tried to show them that we had no intentions of being aggressive. They responded and smiled at us. Dick made them understand that he wanted to trade for some trinkets to take home. They were intent on our rifles and let us know they would like to handle them and see how they worked.

I said no, they couldn't touch our rifles. When I fired at a coconut on a tree, they were impressed. I wasn't sure if they would harm us, but the situation didn't feel right.

Then they brought out a big wooden bowl and sat down. Whatever was in the bowl was white, and they wanted us to eat with them. They dipped in two fingers and put the white mixture in their mouths. It was really disgusting. They chewed betel nut and their mouths and teeth were red. It was revolting to eat out of the same bowl, but we didn't want to offend them. Some women came out to see what was going on. They were bare chested, some of them had babies at their breasts. This eating ritual lasted a while. The natives were trying to negotiate and convince us they wanted to trade. We gave them some rations and they gave Dick some little beads. At first I had thought they were really friendly but thank God I sensed there was something wrong. That was our first campaign. Being two greenhorns in the jungle, we didn't know the

Trading partners in New Guinea

ways of the natives, but I knew it just didn't feel right.

The natives were acting much friendlier, but we realized they were gradually crowding us. I got very uneasy and told Dick, "We have to get out of here, this isn't looking good." He panicked a bit because they were making motions that they wanted his rifle. They knew I wasn't going to give up mine because I made it quite clear there was no way in the world they were even going to touch it. Dick thought we would antagonize them if we didn't give in, and he started to hand over his rifle. I told him if he did, I would shoot him right there because we would be dead anyway. They would kill us if they got our rifles. He finally realized how serious the situation was. I told him, "We're going to back out of here, and whatever

54

you do, don't you dare put your rifle down. You just point it right at them and let them know that if they come at us we'll shoot them." He finally got enough courage to stand up with me and we started backing off.

They were coming toward us aggressively and now they were starting to shout and thrust their spears at us. I shot into the ground to startle them. They stopped and drew back, but then they started to shout again. I told Dick, "Just don't lose your cool, we have to get out of here." We got to an area at the edge of the village where they were making dugout canoes by chipping out logs. I told Dick we'd go out beyond the logs, and once we got on the trail, we'd have to move at a fast pace, but let's not run. I thought if we started to run they might get more aggressive because they would think we were afraid. He kept his mouth shut and I was making it known that if they so much as touched us, there would be a force of our Army troops that would come up here and burn down the village. Eventually, we got far enough down the trail so that we thought it was safe. They followed us for a while and threw some spears at us. Luckily, they were afraid of our rifles, and we did have grenades with us, too. They were saving face by showing us that they were driving us off.

We finally got back close to camp, and we met a five-man patrol on the trail. They had been sent out to find us. We told them what had happened and the sergeant in charge said, "You young shits, you could have been in one of their pots!" I didn't know if he was exaggerating or not, but he said the natives were head-hunters. He was so mad, he said we should go up and burn down the goddamned village. We told him they hadn't harmed us, they just threatened us a little. Later, we described this as our adventure with the "fuzzy-wuzzies." ★

My father Danielle Mancini, age 17 (center)

*My mother (standing), age 21;
Aunt Mary, age 20*

My Uncle Peter (R), who gave me advice.

Mama, brother Bill, and me, age 4

1943 Family gathering, week before Army

1943 Brother-in-law, Mario Frati

1946 My first leave home from the hospital

Joe Verga (L), Moe Cohen (R) Occupation duty in Japan

1946 With my high school friend, Joe Benfante

1946 Recuperating at home on a weekend leave

1950 Dave Mancini, student at
Rochester Institute of Technology

June 17, 1950. Rose and Dave Mancini

1951 My graduation party
from RIT

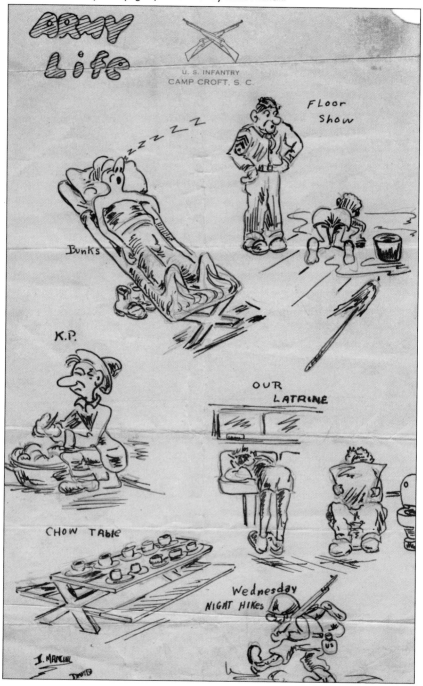

FOR —
DAVID MANCINI
HALLORAN GENI. HOSP.
12 - 23 -45
BEATRICE FUSILLO

Beatrice Fusillo was an art student from Pratt Institute.
During the Christmas season, she sketched portraits for the
hospitalized GIs to send home to their families.

Dutch New Guinea – Fly Trap

At one of our compounds the latrine was set up in a tent. To get to it, you had to go across a man-made foot bridge. When you go to the latrine in the jungle, the flies will eat you alive. To distract the flies, there was a fly trap set up. The fly trap holds leftover food to attract the flies and keep them away from the latrine. One evening I made the trip over to the latrine, and as I was doing my business I sensed movement. I looked over by the fly trap, and there crouched a scrawny little Jap, eating the mess from the fly trap. I thought, "Holy shit!" I was scared, but I could see that he was just as scared as I was. We had been clearing the area of the enemy, and he must have been a straggler who was left behind. He was emaciated, dressed in rags.

He looked at me, and I looked at him. He didn't have a weapon, and neither did I. I probably should have called the corporal of the guard. But I looked at the poor bastard and felt so sorry for him that I gave him a little smile. He gave me a smile and took off. I felt so sorry for him – a guy who was so desperate that he would eat food out of a fly trap. I felt so bad that I told the chaplain about it. I couldn't have anybody kill the poor bastard. He was just trying to survive. I saved some of my rations and left it there that night hoping he would come back and eat it. Shortly after that we shipped out.

In the face of all the horror, there were still moments of man's humanity to man. ★

Dutch New Guinea –
Two Scouts on Parallel Paths

After my first campaign, I ran into my friend Moe Cohen and learned that he had decided to get out of the communications company. He befriended a Sergeant Ted Kalem ("Kimo"), who was the head of Headquarters Intelligence Company, and told him he'd like to become an intelligence and reconnaissance scout. In those days there weren't many people who had graduated from high school. Anybody with a fairly decent IQ was given special assignments, and the sergeant was glad to bring him in. So Moe became part of Headquarters Company in the 3rd Battalion. I was in the 1st Battalion. (Later, in civilian life, Ted Kalem became associate editor and drama critic for TIME magazine.)

Moe hadn't gone through previous training like I had at Camp Croft, so it was on-the-job training for Moe. Moe didn't like to take orders so he liked the idea that as a scout you were pretty independent. I always liked to think that he was jealous of me because I was in the cloak-and-dagger part of the Army and he was just running wire. Moe would later find out that it wasn't so glamorous. You were often sent out to draw enemy fire and expose their location. When Moe was sent out on patrol with a radio man and a couple of scouts, they ran into a Japanese patrol and Moe was wounded.

The interesting thing was, we wound up in similar situations and we were both wounded. Our careers paralleled so closely that we were both wounded near Davao on the Island of Mindanao. Of course, I had to eclipse his dramatic act and get a million dollar wound. Moe was sent back to his outfit and I was sent back to the States.

In spite of all my kidding, Moe was one damned good soldier.

P.S. I always knew when Moe was around. Before he would actually appear, he would always pull some practical joke on me. During a rest period in Goodenough Island, I had my hammock strung and he loosened the ties so that when I got in, it collapsed. I could always hear that guttural laugh. I'd pretend to be pissed. Of course, I was ecstatic to lay eyes on him. ★

Dutch New Guinea – Target Practice

The guys decided they wanted a roast. They spotted something that looked like an antelope, and they started running up this hill and stalking it. One or two of the guys were firing. Before we knew it, a whole platoon was firing. They really put some firepower out there and they never even hit the thing. The sergeant looked up and said, "What the hell is going on here? If that's the way you've been shooting, we haven't killed a Jap yet!" ★

Dutch New Guinea – Learning a Trade and Breaking a Monopoly

My first experience as a barber took place in Dutch New Guinea. We were finishing a mop-up operation since most of the enemy had scattered into the interior. We began to relax and we started to pay attention to our grooming – washing clothes, sewing tatters, shaving, and getting haircuts. We had a professional barber in our outfit. Foreseeing the need for haircuts, he brought along in his pack hand-clippers, scissors, combs, a straight razor, and strap. He was quite entrepreneurial and we were happy to have him.

I've noticed, in my experience in business, that people who are successful seem to turn a little greedy before they straighten themselves out. Then there are those others who take advantage of the unfortunate – the opportunists. Our barber started out charging 50¢ a haircut, which doesn't sound like much, but when you're only getting about $70 a month, every penny counts. But business had become so good for him that he decided to raise his price. We found out through the grapevine that he intended to raise it to a dollar a haircut. There was a little grumbling in the company, and this young private from Brooklyn by the name of Bracco came to me and said the barber was just going to keep raising the price on us, and Bracco refused to pay it. I told him that if he could find a pair of scissors and a comb for me, I'd give him a haircut. He said, "You think you could do it?" I told him, "I know I can do it. My father always cut our hair and I always watched him." He said, "I'll get it for you, Baby."

In a short time he brought back a scissors and comb and I set him up and cut his hair. Before I knew it, I had quite a clientele. And the barber got antsy, because he was losing the business. (By the way, I gave better haircuts than he did

59

because he treated it like an assembly line. He only gave brush cuts, but I took time with the guys and cut their hair to order.) The barber came to me and said, "What the hell are you charging for a haircut?" I told him, "I'm not charging anything." He stood there, shocked. Before he could speak, I said, "I'm doing it because you're a thief. You've got these guys in a hole and you think you can get away running your monopoly. I'll cut them forever for nothing as long as you keep raising your price." He said, "Wait a minute, can't we talk about this?" I told him, "There's nothing to talk about, but I'll tell you what I want. You bring your price down to 50¢ again and I get my haircuts free from you." He agreed.

After that, I still took care of a few people who liked the way I cut their hair, but my barber days were over. I just kept my hand in for my special friends. And I wore a brush cut. ★

Goodenough Island – Another Nickname

If the war didn't get you, Goodenough Island might. When we first arrived, it was terrible. Some guys died from typhus. There were lizards and mice and rats. We burned the underbrush to rid the place of the vermin. One guy survived typhus and came back to us. His hair had turned white from the high fever. Most of the guys who contracted typhus never returned but instead were sent home or died.

The 19th Infantry was regrouping, waiting for reinforcements, more or less licking our wounds. In the short time we were there, the Air Corps had set up a screen to show movies. Many nights we relaxed while watching movies and there was really no fear of any immediate fighting. But the Japanese had a nasty habit of sending over one lone plane, which we called Twelve O'Clock Charlie. Right at 12:00 we could hear the drone of his motor and he would drop a couple of bombs to scatter us and harass us.

After the first run I happened to be sitting down with some of my buddies in the audience watching the movie. When he came over again, we all scattered. I couldn't understand why everyone was running out in the field for cover when there were these big holes on the side of the road. It was just a mystery to me why they would run so far. Why not just jump in a hole? So when we heard Charlie, thinking that I was so smart, I just jumped right in and quickly discovered why everyone was avoiding those big holes. I found myself covered with human waste. That's where natives put their human waste that they used for fertilizer and it was just sitting there, fermenting. I now had my third nickname.

#1 "Baby"   #2 "Superman"   #3 "Shitty"

While other soldiers were getting medals for bravery, I was collecting nicknames. ★

Goodenough Island – I Am Introduced to Tokyo Rose

The first time I met Tokyo Rose, we were in a staging area for our next invasion of one of the islands. A young private from Brooklyn named Bracco said, "You want to hear some really good music?" Of course I was into Sinatra and Glenn Miller, so I said sure, I'd like to hear it. They played around with the radio and managed to get this station, and out came a woman's voice asking, "Are you having a good time?" Some music was playing. One song I remember in particular was "Every Night About This Time" by the Ink Spots. Her voice was very sweet and she said hello to the GIs and welcome to her radio station. One of the guys said it was Tokyo Rose. It was the first time I ever heard her.

> "Her voice was very sweet and she said hello to the GIs..."

The propaganda was geared to destroy our morale, but if anything, it built up our morale because it made us want to get the war over sooner and get back to our loved ones. At least that's the incentive it gave me. I know that later on she was called a war criminal, but I'm not sure we shouldn't have given her some kind of a medal. She certainly helped my morale. Without her I never would have listened to Glenn Miller or have heard any of the new songs that were coming out. ★

Shipboard to the Invasion of Leyte

We were on our way to the invasion of Leyte, and from our departure point it was about a two-day trip. I made friends with a young black sailor who had access to the ship's food supplies. I remember that he was small and had a round face. We promised to write to one another. He served the officers, and he sneaked out cans of fruit and fruit cocktail for me, and I replaced my K rations with the fruit. I was devastated, and still am, that my little friend's ship was blown up in the harbor during the assault, and he was killed.

In the first days of fighting on Leyte, all I ate was canned fruit, fruit cocktail, and chocolate bars, and drank water. The chocolate bars were interesting. If you ate a piece, you became bloated like you were pregnant. They blew up in your stomach to keep you full. The biscuits were similar. If you dropped them into water, they would blow up to the size of a frying pan. Just another way to placate a ravenous GI.

One day I was up on deck topside and overheard a loud argument. Gambling was one of the distractions and a favorite pastime of the soldiers. There was a big gambling game going on and a fight broke out. A guy was trying to defend himself. Two guys were holding him and another guy was about to pound him, demanding his money back. I realized that I knew the guy who was in trouble. It was a guy from Rochester, my hometown. I stepped in and first tried to calm them down, but they told me to stay out of it: "This cheating SOB is either going to pay us back or we're going to throw him overboard."

Fortunately, I had some money on me, and together we managed to pay the two soldiers he had cheated. When I questioned him, he admitted he had cheated. He said to me, "What the hell, we're going into combat. I was just trying to have some fun." I am not so sure it was "trying to have fun," or just his larcenous nature. He promised to pay me back.

At dawn the next day we were going down the nets for the invasion. I didn't see him again until almost the end of the Leyte campaign, and afterwards I didn't see him until we were both discharged. By the way, he did pay back the money he borrowed. ★

Leyte – Beach Landing, October 19, 1944

When our troop ship arrived off the shores of Leyte, we could still see the planes from the carriers strafing and bombing and dumping firebombs. The cruisers sitting out in the bay were shelling the hell out of the island. When the cruisers stopped, the destroyers shelled. The island looked like a big fireball. Of course, we liked it because we had a gut feeling that the bombardment was blowing the whole Japanese army away. The inferno would clear them out and we would

meet very little resistance. We were now assembling on deck, and groups of us started climbing down the rope nets to our assigned landing craft. The LCs were bobbing up and down, and one of the perils of climbing down the nets was that you had to time your jump just right. The waves were driving the landing craft up against the ship. If you misjudged when to drop, you could be crushed. These were the assault waves.

Once we were on the LCs, we circled to rendezvous. We were in a line, like a race. I remember the lieutenant saying to the coxswain, "You watch that flag, and when that flag goes down, we race for the beach. And I don't want you dropping us off in the middle of the water. You'd better drive this goddamned thing onto the beach. If you hesitate, I'll shoot you." (Some guys drowned at Tarawa because the landing craft dropped them off at high tide.) As we were rendezvousing, the last bunch of LCIs with rockets on them ran across the front of the island and fired point blank. We cheered, because we figured nothing could live through that and we would be able to waltz onto the beach after that last assault. The firepower was so intense that the smell of gunpowder and explosives almost made you sick. But on the other hand, it gave us courage, knowing this was being done. The beach might be easier to land on.

As we came in closer to the beach, I spotted poles in the water. I couldn't figure out what they were, but the Japanese had set them out there to zero in on us with their mortars and artillery. They knew that once we had passed the poles, they were zeroed in on our landing crafts. We saw some of our landing crafts being blown up once they passed the target poles. Our LC started to run full speed and it was a race to get to the beach. There were planes constantly passing overhead. You felt it in the pit of your stomach. We were all so scared that our officers had given us slices of oranges to suck on so we wouldn't throw up. Whoever tells you they aren't frightened during an assault is full of shit, or just plain crazy.

I've never experienced the feeling of wanting to get out of anything so badly. Before the ramp drops and you're about to hit the beach, it's a mass of humanity pressing forward hard against one another. The enemy fire is coming down – it's almost like being in a hailstorm. You're pushing and shoving to get out. You're annoyed and claustrophobic with all those bodies around you. You feel anger toward your own men. You long for space and air. It seems like an eternity – no one is moving. You know the longer you stay there, the bigger the target you become. Once the ramp goes down, you feel a sense of relief and you go charging out.

In a landing there are two times that you feel fear, your stomach is queasy, and there's a feeling of panic. The first time is going down the net, because it's the beginning of the unknown. The second time is when we are all waiting to hit the beach and there are bodies pressing up against the ramp. You're overwhelmed by an almost suffocating feeling of claustrophobia. You feel like you want to explode out of a box.

When the ramp dropped, the officer didn't even have

to tell us to charge. Unfortunately, I stepped into a depression in the sand and started going under water. I grabbed the soldier in front of me, and he tried to beat me off with his rifle because he didn't need my extra weight. I was carrying a radio, and with the weight of the equipment I was wearing, I would have drowned right there if I hadn't hung onto him. As soon as he pulled me out of the hole, we charged in and started crawling on the beach on our bellies. I crawled into a shell hole and another teenage soldier ended up in the hole with me. I called him Buddy. I didn't know him, but when you're in a hole like that under assault conditions, you're pretty close. He was shaking like a leaf. We had cover, but we couldn't stay there very long because the Japanese were starting to zero in on the beach with mortars and machine gun fire. We had to get under cover of the jungle. I told Buddy that after the next barrage we had to move out fast because the Japs were starting to zero in. He shook his head and could hardly speak or move. He was paralyzed with fear. I tried to convince him but finally said, "Screw you, I'm going!" I ran into the jungle and immediately felt safer there under cover of the foliage. I could see the beach being blasted. When it let up a little, I went back out and tried again to convince Buddy to come with me, but he froze. He couldn't move. He motioned to leave him alone, so I told him one last time, "I'm leaving."

As we were moving in toward the jungle, I encountered an officer. He told me to see if I could move up forward and draw some fire to see where the enemy was. I said, "Yes, sir." In the confusion on the beach our outfits had become separated. He didn't know me and I didn't know him, so I thought, *screw you*! I'm not drawing fire. My conscience bothered me about this kid Buddy, so I circled around and went back to the beach to look for him. When I reached the area, I found him dead and almost decapitated. I cried and felt guilty that I had let him down. My mother taught me that I was my brother's keeper. You never leave anyone behind. I still feel guilty that I didn't just knock him out and drag him, whether he liked it or not.

In the middle of the night we were still trapped on the 67

beaches. There were Japanese running between us and the jungle. Our guys couldn't get tanks in there for us. Somehow, the Seabees brought in bulldozers and we advanced with the blades in front of us. I looked back when I got to the edge of the jungle and the bodies of GIs were strewn everywhere. I'll never forget that endless sight of death. As we pushed forward, the resistance was heavy. But as the bulldozers advanced and covered up the Japanese pillboxes, the Japanese would dig themselves out and shoot at us. In response our guys brought in flamethrowers to flush the Japanese out of their holes and hiding places. After the flamethrowers I saw Japanese corpses scattered everywhere. That's when I realized that whether we liked it or not, we all died together.

Incidentally, the only time we fought alongside black soldiers was during the invasion of Leyte. We fought for three weeks. During that time four black guys were sent to the front lines for punishment. It seems they had been unloading ships and were fooling around, so they were sent to fight with us. They were scared to death. We'd been fighting long enough that we were conditioned to know when bullets were going over our heads, but it was all new to them. One guy was funny. He couldn't wait to get out of there. The way he put it was, "I'll never ignore an order again. Not even for my wife. I can always get another wife, but I can never get another life!"

Sadly, the black man was considered inferior, so of course the Army hesitated to use them in front line combat. They challenged their bravery and intelligence, and questioned their ability to perform under fire, even though they had proven themselves over and over again, dating back to our Civil War between the States. The record of the Tuskegee pilots in World War II, the all-black unit that performed with valor and distinction, speaks for itself. Since WWII, in Korea, Vietnam, Desert Storm, and Iraq – if not for the minority soldier, especially the African-American, there would be no American Army as we know it today. ★

Leyte – The Aroma of War

In jungle warfare, your senses are awakened to a high intensity. You are aware of everything or you don't survive. I found that my sense of smell was so keen that at times it became more important than my eyesight. The veterans used to tell us that if you're lucky enough to survive the first campaign, as you go along to other battles your instincts and senses sharpen and your chances for survival become better. In jungle warfare the enemy could be only a few yards away from you, and your instincts have to be keen enough to sense that. Nature's natural radar in your body will help you survive. I became aware of this transition in me after the invasion of Leyte. At that point I guess I could say I, too, was now a veteran. I was no longer a kid.

The aroma of warfare lives with me until this day. I could smell my surroundings, I could smell death, I could smell the enemy, I could smell the civilians, I could smell my comrades, I could smell fear. The stench of decomposing bodies mingled with the smell of gunpowder and explosives is unlike any other. It makes you sick to your stomach. All these scents blended into one to become a permanent stench that is etched in my memory forever.

For example, when I went on my first family picnic (Durand Eastman Park in Rochester, NY) after returning Stateside, we were hiking along a trail. The smell of the woods – the rotting trees and vegetation, the musty smell from water-soaked logs and rotting leaves – brought back frightening memories. To this day in certain situations when different aromas flicker around my nostrils, my mind reverts back to the smell of bloating bodies. Time is no cure for the trauma that is experienced in war.

I'm not so sure that in times of need we don't revert back to our ancestors' instincts to survive. ★

Leyte, October 19–20, 1944 – Refugees From War

The 24th Division was assigned the mission of attacking the Japanese left flank as we moved toward the interior of the Island of Leyte. The 19th Infantry was in the forward position of the assault attack. Our sister regiment was on the left, and the third regiment was in reserve. We moved up to capture the high ground and were ordered to take the hill – Hill 522 – at all cost. I was in the assault wave. The 19th took the brunt of the attack. We secured a foothold, but we met a very stubborn enemy and we paid the price in casualties. In order to hold the hill, the reserve regiment moved through us and continued to push the enemy back. The 19th had many dead and wounded soldiers, so we were pulled back in reserve to be reinforced with fresh recruits.

It was the monsoon season, and the rain was coming down in sheets. When our battalion (the 1st Battalion) got to the reserve area, we were stationed around an artillery battery of 105s and 155s. The Japs were infiltrating our lines and sending suicide missions to destroy the guns. Normally, I would be out scouting, but I was put on guard in the outer perimeter that night to protect the guns. It was a makeshift situation, we hadn't even strung barbed wire but had just mostly lain booby traps.

The rain was a deluge. It was a typical tropical storm. The convergence of cold rain and hot jungle floor created a mist that shrouded everything. I dragged pieces of logs into my foxhole, but I was still lying in water. My vision was blurred by the rain and the mist, and it was pitch black when the place wasn't lit up by Japanese mortars and the flash from our big guns.

In the flash of the gunfire, I caught a glimpse of a shadow. It was moving, and I thought it was the enemy, but it was very small. Suddenly, I realized it was a little boy running through the booby-trapped field. I could hear him sobbing, almost hysterical. I crawled out of my foxhole. Afraid of the booby traps we'd lain, I worked my way very carefully out to where he was. I put my hands up in a "stay still" gesture, and he stopped. I was afraid he'd be blown up. It's a miracle he hadn't been killed in the crossfire. When I reached the boy, I grabbed him and carried him back to my foxhole, making sure that I took the same route.

Back in my foxhole I tried to protect him by wrapping him with a poncho. The only way I could keep him out of the water was to have him lie on my chest. Eventually he fell asleep, clinging to me. I held him trembling in my arms all night long. Most of the time I tried not to move because I didn't want to wake him up, and I remember feeling my legs begin to cramp. The rain never quit. To keep the water from getting too deep, I used my helmet to bail and just wore the liner. Our artillery batteries fired all night long, laying a barrage to keep the Japanese from counterattacking. It was like daylight most of the time because of the flashes from the big guns and the Japanese mortars that were dropping

Nature's Washtub - Foxhole

in on us. In a way, we were fortunate that the rain came down so heavily. We were bogged down but the enemy was, too. I tried to stay alert, and there was no movement other than the firing back and forth of heavy weapons.

In the morning I looked at my little friend and saw that he was covered with sores. He was so tiny and frail, and so miserable. His sores were weeping badly and I couldn't bear to see the pain in his eyes, so I carried him to an aid station. (In Korea, it was called a MASH station, where the wounded were cared for before they were shipped back to the rear echelon.) The doctor questioned me, "What have you got there?" He was busy with the casualties and he seemed a little annoyed. But I was so weary that his attitude made me

71

kind of mad. I told him, "I've got a little kid who seems to be covered with sores." He took a look and told me the boy had a bad case of jungle ulcers - large, weeping sores. He gave some orders and when I left, he and a male nurse were washing the ulcers so they could medicate them. I told the boy that I would be back to see him. The next day he was in much better spirits. Speaking broken English, he let us know he was worried about his sister. He said he had lost her. He didn't seem to be able to answer questions about his

Perla

parents. He was confused and scared and kept talking about his sister.

Two days later, I ran into a young girl who was asking if anyone had seen her brother. She said she'd lost her family, and her little brother was all she had left. When the bombardment started he panicked and ran, and she couldn't find him in the dark. I told her I'd found a little boy, and took her to the aid station. He shouted when he saw her. They were hugging each other, crying and happy, and I walked away.

It turned out that they kept the boy at the aid station, and his sister was so grateful that she "adopted" me. She called me her "edoi" and would bring me rice and fried fish as her way of thanking me. I realized she was so thankful that she was depriving herself of food. She even tried to wash my fatigues and clothes. Her name was Perla. On one visit to our camp, she brought a couple of girls with her. She apologized to me but she wondered if I could give them some food. Since I was willing to trade all my beer and cigarette rations for food, I usually had all the food I could handle. Any extra food I gave to Perla and her friends.

After about two weeks, Perla somehow learned that we were about to have a troop movement and she surmised

that I was going to leave. She came to me with tears stream-
ing down her face. She could barely speak, but she finally
blurted out that she wanted to have a baby by me so she
would never forget me. She said I would forget her. I gave
her all the pesos I had in my pocket and all the food I could
get my hands on that day. She was
so grateful that I had saved her
brother. He was the only link she
had to her past, and she wanted to
hold on to me hoping that there
would be a future for her. But
war kills the future and destroys
the past. She told me, "War is so
terrible. But I wouldn't have found
you if we hadn't had the war. So
in a way, I lost my loved ones but they were replaced by
you. I will never see you again, but I will never forget you."

> "I realized she
> was so thankful
> that she was
> depriving herself
> of food."

     She was so right. Time fades your memory. I went
back to the front lines and I never saw her again. People
wonder why soldiers are tormented with bad dreams, and
why we are so opposed to war. But events like this are
seared in our memories like mental tattoos. ★

Leyte – Fighting the Elements and Corruption

After a quiet day of scouting, I settled down in my foxhole to spend a hot evening. I had opened my shirt and was sitting back trying to relax. Suddenly I felt something crawl across the lower part of my neck and down my shirt. I sat very still, and when it got to a certain point, I figured I'd crush it. I pounded myself as hard as I could, but it had no effect on the intruder. I felt a severe puncture, and then the most awful burning sensation I have ever experienced in my life. I ripped off my shirt and flung it, and discovered that I'd been attacked by a very large centipede. Almost immediately I got sick to my stomach. I felt awful, and was nauseous and feverish all night. I didn't dare get out of the foxhole at night, so the next day I sought out the aid man and showed him the marks left by the centipede. I had a welt and it looked like something had stuck me. He wasn't very sympathetic. He said, "If you lived through the night, you'll be ok now."

Days later, I was out on another scouting mission. It was quite late when I returned and in the darkness I somehow encountered a spider. I have no idea what kind of spider it was, but it was quite large and it bit me on the side of the head next to my temple. My whole face began to swell up and my eye was almost immediately swollen shut. When the guys saw me, they said I'd better get over to the aid station. But when I got to the aid station, the doctor (a captain) wouldn't come out to look at me. Apparently he had had a bad day tending to the wounded. I called him a "no good sonofabitch." He asked my name and I said, "Fuck you!" He said he'd find out who I was. The next day he came looking for me. I was trying to bathe my eye. I told my commanding officer what had happened and that this captain wouldn't tend to me and wanted to punish me. The CO confronted the captain and said, "You mean to tell me you couldn't get out of your bunk and take care of this kid?"

I was swollen down the side of my neck and up my face. The doctor said I had insulted an officer and I was insubordinate. The CO sent him packing, and he had another medic look at me. They cleaned the bite and gave me some pills, hoping the swelling would subside. The worst part of this incident was that they wouldn't send me back to the rear lines. I couldn't go scouting because I couldn't see. We were moving up, advancing on the enemy. So, here I was in a combat situation, trying to travel with one eye swollen shut and the other one weeping. It was really squirrelly. I felt like I needed a guide dog.

> *He asked my name and I said, "Fuck you!"*

Another mishap was that I contracted malaria. I was delirious for a week. I was in a foxhole, and they wouldn't send me back for treatment. They just kept loading me with pills. Finally my fever broke. I had a malaria attack again after I got back to the States. They say it never completely leaves your system.

I managed to get myself punished and sent back to the front lines during one brief respite. We discovered that people in the quartermaster were selling our American rations to the Australians, and getting cheap rations that they would then feed to us. There was an officer who was making a lot of money at this. We wrote a letter to Congress explaining what was happening. My officer okayed the letter, but it was intercepted by the censors and we got in trouble. We were worn out and supposed to have a week's rest period, but we were sent back to the front lines for punishment. Of course, our letter never went anywhere. After that experience I learned to question a lot more things about the war. ★

Leyte -The Wild, Wild West Comes to Leyte

One of our very first casualties after the beachhead and securing the surrounding hills was one of our Oklahoma cowboys. We came across a couple of water buffalo. This Oklahoma wiseass decided to try to ride one. He always claimed that back home he rode Brahma bulls. He got hold of one of the buffalo, leaped on it, and before he knew what happened, he was flat on his back.

He received a "million dollar wound" without ever firing a shot. The medics thought he broke his back, and we never saw him again. The platoon sergeant was so pissed off! He laid down the law: "I don't want to see any more cowboy shit. And that's an order!" ★

Leyte – Hand–to–Hand Combat

During one of our overnight bivouacs, we had established a perimeter around some heavy mortars and machine guns. The Japanese were putting a lot of pressure on our perimeters by sneaking in and infiltrating us at night. They would use a knife to kill you in your foxhole and sneak back out. It was becoming very common that almost every night we would catch one in our perimeter and kill him, or we'd find some dead GIs in their foxholes. During this period, one sergeant said that to avoid us shooting one another, we had to have a password. Whenever they discovered someone in the perimeter, the sergeant would go from hole to hole and call the password. If you didn't answer, he would just shoot.

With my luck, it happened one evening that a Japanese soldier broke into my foxhole and we started to struggle. I hollered out to let everyone know the enemy was in our perimeter and while we were fighting, the sergeant came up to the hole. He kept shouting at me, "Push him away from you! Push him away from you! Goddamn it, Baby, kick the sonofabitch away from you!" When I finally got my feet up against his body and pushed him back, the sergeant just blasted him. That was my first hand-to-hand combat experience. ★

Leyte – Hill 522 and Palo
October 29, 1944

We pushed off the beaches of Leyte, and our assignment was to secure Hill 522. Whoever held 522 controlled the beaches and the surrounding area. During the night we lost communication with one of our battalions (I believe it was the 3rd Battalion). We had prearranged passwords should it become necessary to use them. It was dusk, and I had scouted the area and was familiar with it, so I was volunteered to try to contact the 3rd Battalion and bring them a radio or field phone. While I was working my way to the left, I realized there was a nest of Japanese. I could hear them talking. I quietly squirmed my way through their lines and somehow I was fortunate enough to not be detected. My biggest problem as I worked my way up to the 3rd Battalion was whether someone had changed the password. As luck would have it, it was the same password they had assigned to us earlier, and they realized I wasn't one of the enemy and let me in. Then we had communication again and it made it easier for us to assault the hill.

Liberation does not bring happiness

A battery of artillery and heavy mortars was saturating the hill with steady bombardment. When they stopped firing, we fixed bayonets and charged up the hill. Fortunately for us, many of our airplanes, Navy Corsairs, had been strafing and bombing the hill. When we finally took the hill we found many tunnels, but the Japanese who didn't retreat were dazed and unable to resist, and we took the hill.

We rested there for a full day, and the next morning we started moving out to the town of Palo. From our vantage point we could look down with our field glasses and see the Japanese milling around down there, setting up fortifications to hold us off. This was the route to move on into the Ormoc Valley and the interior of Leyte, and they knew we were coming down. We called for more air strikes and artillery bombardment and with more heavy fighting, we took Palo.

Events of this particular battle affected some of the young soldiers, like myself, more than we realized. After the first battle where we drove them out, the Japanese counterattacked that night. They dressed up in their ceremonial uniforms. They blared music, and all of a sudden they shouted "Banzai" and they attacked us in waves. They overran our perimeters. I took cover under a 3/4-ton truck and was behind a wheel, firing. A young private from Connecticut held off the counterattack at a bridge by firing a machine gun to the point where his ammunition was gone and the barrel was so hot you couldn't touch it. The young private was called a hero and promoted to corporal in a heavy weapons company.

> "The Japanese bodies were stacked at the bridge, their lives snuffed out."

When some of the officers congratulated him, he had no idea what he had done. Talking to him later, he said that he really didn't know what he'd done, he just froze on the trigger and kept firing. Known to us as a friendly kid, he never talked much after that and you rarely saw him smile. Casualties were high on both sides. The Japanese bodies were stacked at the bridge, their lives snuffed out. No matter who wins or loses in war, everyone is a loser because the war devastates both sides. Ironically, after our first campaign the veterans told us, "You've earned your stripe and you're now men." They called it baptism under fire. But what they forgot to add was that we'd lost our youth and innocence.

Even more devastating to me than the battles we fought was the scene when we went into village after village where friendly fire and Japanese fire had reaped a slaughter. We stopped the air strikes and lifted our artillery bombardment when we moved in to liberate Palo, and that's when we found the destruction. The bodies of babies, mothers, young girls, and boys were lying all around. The villagers had sought sanctuary in their church, but it suffered a direct hit. There were dead bodies everywhere. I was affected by losing some of my friends on the beach, but I think I was more deeply affected by seeing the defenseless women, and especially the innocent children, whose lives had just been senselessly extinguished. There was no bringing them back. They were gone forever.

Church in Palo (Leyte)

When the battle was over, my duty was to scout and try to get information from the enemy dead or interrogate the prisoners. This took me into the area of these dead bodies. Bleeding mothers held their dead babies, trying to shelter them even though they were dead in their arms. Worse yet was the sight of small children trying to wake up their dead mothers. I broke down and cried. I couldn't believe that man could be so cruel. I remember shouting, looking up into heaven and asking, "Where are you? If you are our Father and we are your children, how can you allow this to happen to us?"

Later on, when we had secured the area, there were children and mothers who wouldn't let go of the dead, holding onto their bodies as though they were trying to breathe life back into them. One of the cruelest and hardest things to do was to take that dead loved one away and try to help them understand that they were gone forever. The one chaplain we had with us was overcome with grief.

Sometimes the cost of liberty is worse than being occupied. Knowing the true consequences of war, if an individual were given a choice, I wonder which one he would choose. ★

Battle of Pastrana – Nov. 11, 1944

While we were slugging our way toward Pastrana, we got bogged down and couldn't advance any further. Our artillery hadn't moved up far enough to be within range of our fighting and we couldn't call in for air strikes because the weather was bad. God was on our side, but I wondered where he was. The enemy was against us and so was the weather. It seemed as though we could never get dry. The ground surface was generally deep mud and slime. We were perfect candidates for jungle rot, malaria, jungle ulcers, and dysentery. We had light mortars, but we needed more firepower, so we radioed in for 4.2 mortars to come up. The colonel in charge was so gung ho and anxious to get more medals that despite our dilemma, he insisted we move up and take Pastrana.

Before we could advance, they needed intelligence on the situation. That was the job of the scouts. Sometimes scouts were sent out in patrols of three or four, but occasionally we would separate, depending on the situation. It was heartbreaking when one of us did not return. This was a good reason for not getting too close to your comrades.[1] Three of us were sent to see if we could find out what was up ahead. I was sent to the left, and I cautiously crawled my way through the high Kunai grass. I kept very low until I reached the town. I was very surprised that it was so quiet. There wasn't a sound. My skin was crawling with tension because I sensed the enemy was letting us in. They were watching me. If they could make me think the area was deserted, I'd give a false report.

We found out later that the Japanese had actually built pillboxes underneath the village huts and reinforced them with palm trees, earth, and concrete. They used the tall Kunai grass to camouflage the pillboxes. I had never seen Kunai grass growing so close to the huts. The Filipinos always cleaned it away so they could plant gardens. The children would play underneath the huts and chickens ran around there, too. So it was strange to me to see all the grass around the huts. It looked unusual. That's when I became suspicious, and had a crawly feeling that something wasn't right. At one point I got down on one knee and tried to look around, and at the same time keep a low silhouette in case someone wanted to take a shot at me. I felt something hot under my knee, like there had been a fire not too long ago and it had been covered up with sand. That's when I knew for sure that the Japanese were setting me up to report false information. I was their patsy.

Rather than run, I just slowly backed off. When I got to the edge of the Kunai grass in the jungle, I started running. The strange part of it was that they had snipers, and not one of them fired at me. When I got back, my lieutenant was waiting for me. The other two scouts had come back early, and he suspected they hadn't gone very far. They reported there was no one there. He told me, "Baby, I'm glad you're back because you've been gone a long time and I know your report will be thorough." I told him what I suspected and what I saw, about the strange grass that was up against the huts. I thought it was camouflage, and bunkers or pillboxes were underneath the huts. He reported to the CP, telling him what I had learned, but the colonel didn't want to hold up the operation. The lieutenant and his captain were suggesting to the colonel that we wait for the 4.2 to come up so we could soften them up. There was no way, if they actually had pillboxes, that we could flush them out without support. This colonel was gung ho and he was determined to win some kind of commendation. He ordered us to move out.

Needless to say, we walked right into the enemy's trap and were repulsed by their heavy fire. They even had small cannons. Their mortar fire and sniper fire were so deadly that we were pinned down. While we were pinned down I ran into my friend, Moe Cohen from Rochester, and we took

cover together. Snipers climbed tall trees and strapped themselves onto branches so they could lie in wait for a long time.
This gave them a clear view of troops moving along trails or
higher ground. All of a sudden I saw movement in a tree quite a
distance away, and I fired. A rifle toppled out and I realized that
I had hit a sniper. Moe congratulated me and pretended he was
jealous that I got my first before he did. I never said anything to
him, but again I regretted that I had taken a life.

Shortly after that, the colonel gave a command to fix bayonets and charge the pillboxes. We lost many men as a result of
his arrogance. If he had exercised some patience and waited for
the 4.2 mortars to come up, we would have saved many lives. In
the end, before we could take the town we had to wait for the
4.2s to direct their fire so they could destroy the Japanese guns.
After the artillery had moved up a little closer and they started to
lob shells, eventually we were able to take the town. It was a
tough fight, and we endured unnecessary loss of life just to feed
the colonel's ego. My only satisfaction was that the colonel was
later relieved of his command by Brigadier General Cramer.

I learned later that it was not uncommon for some of the
officers to play war games just so they could get another star or
medal. I also discovered, the longer I was in the service, that
there were more and more of the high-ranking officers who acted
the same way, including General MacArthur.

On the other hand, I remember the names of two
generals that the GIs spoke of very highly – General Eichelberger[2]
and General Krueger. ★

[1] "To be made a scout in jungle war is somehow akin to being scheduled for death. Good squad
leaders select the best men to serve as scouts. Some, intent on keeping old friends alive, select green
replacements for the job. Most did not live long. But the scout shrugs, wary, unhappy and aggressive.
He knows that in the mystery of jungle growth the enemy can lie in wait and not be seen within a
whisper's reach."

Jan Valtin, Children of Yesterday (Nashville, Battery Press, 1988), p.111

[2] "The huge casualty disparity between the Japanese and Americans is remarkable. The difference was
partly a tribute to the infantry scouts and "sneak patrols" who, at great risk to themselves, forged ahead
and doggedly uncovered enemy ambushes and positions. Given the dense jungle growth, General
Eichelberger remembered, "in the end," the only way to find a Japanese position "was to send in a man
with a gun…and generally for the muddy, thirsty scout warily pushing through thick underbrush, his
first knowledge of a bunker's location was when the enemy soldier in it began firing at him."

Stephen J. Lofgren, Hyperwar: The Southern Philippines (www.ibiblio.org/hyperwar/USA/USA-C-
Sphilippines/index.html), p.35

Leyte — Comrades in Arms

In the battle for Leyte, the weather at times was our worst enemy. In fact, the weather was almost worse than the war. It seemed as though the rain would never stop and the fog would never lift. The terrain was a tangle of wet vines and jungle grass as tall as the natives' huts. Nature had pulled down a curtain of dense mist that surrounded us for days.

Our battalion was short of rations, so our officers called for a supply drop. In order for the cargo planes to make the drop, they sent out spotter planes to find us. When the spotters located us through our radio communications, we threw smoke grenades so they could see where we were. The planes swooped in with food supplies. Unfortunately, under such foul conditions, the drop was slightly off and the rations landed between our lines and the Japanese.

We were all fighting so hard – both the enemy and the GIs. The Japs were trying to hold their position and they hadn't been supplied, either. When the drop came, they charged out to grab some of the supplies and so did we. We just grabbed the food and ran to our perimeter. In many instances both sides could see their enemy, and we didn't even bother to shoot each other. In that brief moment we became comrades in arms. We had called our own truce.

The food was appreciated and wonderful. We carried K rations with us in battle. They were compact and very light, about the size of a small can of tuna fish. We could carry many of them, and one can was a meal. It kept you alive, but it was crap. Instead of the old K rations, we were excited to see that they had dropped C rations. Under combat conditions, C rations are like filet mignon. We had an assortment of canned goods – hot dogs and sauce, meatballs and macaroni, and jelly and biscuits. It was a great treat. But when you stop and think about it, all it did was refuel our energy and I am sure it did theirs, too. We just began all over again. So the food became more ammunition for us to destroy each other. At that point I almost felt — let's just walk away from this. I was wishing somebody would blow a whistle and call the game to an end. We finally were successful and drove them off. ★

Leyte – Bridge

We were advancing pretty fast to reinforce our troops on the other side of the island, after taking Hill 522 and the Ormoc Valley. The Japs were doing everything they could to prevent our advance. We came to a deep ravine with a bridge the Japs had pretty much destroyed. We had to go across it, even though they had blown it apart. The objective was to get as much firepower across as possible. We could hear the firing of a skirmish on the other side of the ravine. There was an option to climb down and back up the other side, if we didn't feel we could cross the bridge, but I was so darned tired that I decided to take my chances on the bridge, even though I was terrified.

All that remained of the structure was some 10-by-10-inch beams on a wooden framework. The crevasse was about 60-70 feet deep, and looking down we could see water and rocks jutting out. What was left of the bridge spanned about 100 feet. Riflemen, ordered to hold a position, had already crossed over with light machine guns. A heavy weapons platoon was going across the bridge; some of the soldiers were carrying machine guns and tripods, and a bunch of us were bringing up the rear.

As we worked our way onto the bridge, one soldier in front of me was carrying a heavy tripod for a .30 caliber machine gun. Suddenly he froze. We were stuck behind him in the middle of the bridge. The other guys started cursing him out. I was immediately behind him. I was shaking to start with, because I was afraid of heights. I had wanted to get it over with, and was determined to temporarily overcome my fear and get across the thing. Now here I was in the middle of nowhere, and exposed to enemy fire. I'd have to climb over him. I managed to lift his tripod off and handed it over to the guy in front of him, who had already taken off his equipment and worked his way back to help.

The frozen kid couldn't get up. We encouraged him to straddle the bridge and try to work his way across sitting down, but his legs were getting hung up on the broken boards. Finally, the other soldier and I maneuvered over him. We got a grip on him and got him up. He managed to hang onto us and we walked him across. To me, it was almost worse than facing the bullets we could hear on the other side. There was no control up there on the bridge at that height. I was scared to death. When I got to the other side, I almost threw up. ★

Leyte – Celebrations and Sorrows, a Beach Party, and the "Immaculate Conception"

Finally, after months of fighting in Leyte, our mail caught up with us. Some of my relatives had sent me canned goods, which were wonderful because they didn't spoil. I had also received a fruit cake. But the most interesting food my relatives sent was provolone cheese and big chunks of salami and pepperoni. When we finally got our packages, they were waterlogged because they had been lying on the beach. Part of the wrapping had been broken open and exposed to the sun and heat as well. We had a pact among us in the platoon that if we got packages of food from home, we would share them. My packages were typically gourmet fare, and everybody was anxious to start eating. People were just cutting off chunks of salami and pepperoni and provolone cheese with their combat knives.

> "My packages were typically gourmet fare, and everybody was anxious to start eating."

We sat there enjoying it as if we were at a fine restaurant. In fact, one of the guys said it was better than the Ritz. Suddenly, one of the guys looked up and said, "What the hell is this? This thing looks like it's crawling." There were maggots in the meat. By now we had already eaten a good portion, so we all said, "To hell with it, it's all meat!" and we continued to enjoy it, worms and all.

Our letters were treasured. Everyone was anxious to hear the news from home. There was good news – children having birthdays and a wife informing her husband that he was a father. There was sad news, too. The "Dear John" letter. The wife filing for divorce because she'd met someone else. This happened quite often. Sometimes the War Department through the Red Cross would notify the GI that his wife had become a mother. Except he had been overseas for 18 months. The "immaculate conception."

There was one guy who was so happy his wife had a baby, and some of the guys were talking, "How the hell could she have a baby when he's been here almost two years." He was enthralled by the blessed event until the truth dawned on him. He went around berating her, "That fucking whore. She couldn't keep her legs closed." When his wife wrote to him, he tore up her letters without opening them. Then she sent him pictures and he finally showed them to us and asked, "Do you think the baby looks like me?" His wife kept writing to him, begging for forgiveness. She said it was a moment of weakness. She was frightened that he'd never come back. He began to mellow a little bit, and I remember him saying, "You can't blame her. I've been screwing around, too. It's not all that bad, is it. When I go home, I have a wife and a son." After he'd reconciled himself to it, he couldn't wait to receive more pictures from home. I don't know what happened to him. As time went on, we were separated. But I hope he found peace and happiness when he finally arrived home and that he really appreciated having a son. ★

Combat Humor

We had just come through a difficult campaign in the Ormoc Valley in the Philippines, with heavy casualties. The 19th Infantry was pulled out into a rest area. Our assignment was to unload Air Corps supplies for the pilots. We would get on a barge early every morning and set out to the ships to unload them. This was considered a rest period from combat. While we were unloading the ships, we discovered that the Air Corps had some special goodies that we combat soldiers never saw, so one of us was always assigned to see how much he could confiscate to bring back and share with the rest of our company.

We always had water cans with us. When we found these large cans of juices – orange, tomato – we would puncture the juice cans with our jungle knives and fill our water cans and canteens with the juices to take back. While unloading one particular ship, we discovered crates of fresh eggs. We took anything that was soft – our underclothes – and wrapped the eggs, and stuffed them into the openings of the water cans. We were very fortunate because we managed to salvage almost all of the eggs, and we had a feast. For a couple of weeks we were stealing everything we could get our hands on. It was wonderful because the Air Corps even had fresh meat that we were able to sneak out. Retrieving the fresh meat was the most difficult and we weren't able to steal much because it was kept in refrigerated containers, which were hard to break into.

We hit the jackpot when one of the soldiers discovered a crate loaded with pilots' watches. We broke into it and when we got back, we gave them to most of our platoon. They were all sporting these beautiful watches. But that became our downfall. When they discovered the watches were gone, they started a search. Although they never found the watches, we were no longer assigned to unload that ship. Instead, we were ordered to unload 90-gallon drums of fuel from another ship. From a cushy job we went to a backbreaking job.

Part of our relaxation was fishing. Lack of proper fishing gear was no problem because we fished with grenades. We'd throw the grenades into the water and the fish would float to the top. We cooked them by greasing the top of a 90-gallon drum. We'd cut off the tails and heads and fry these little fish on the drum. They were delicious.

The lieutenant who was in charge of our assignment approached me one day and said, "Come on, you're coming with me. We need your innocent baby face to do something." I asked what was up, and he said we were going to steal a coffin with six holes in it. (A coffin is a latrine box.) He had a big truck waiting and five of us piled in. We wrote up a phony order. He said, "I'll talk to this officer and tell him we're here to pick up this thing from the engineers." We drove in, and while I talked to this GI who was guarding this area and kept him busy, the lieutenant conducted his business.

I offered this guy a so-called authentic Japanese flag. Actually, it was a phony that I had made. We'd gotten some Japanese silk from their parachutes and we had captured a Japanese flag. I took the measurements and we cut out flags. Being an artist, I had copied the Japanese wording and then I made a stencil and stenciled a flag, complete with the red ball. While I kept the guard occupied, we took the coffin. We put it on the truck and drove away.

We unloaded the truck when we got back to camp. Incidentally, we did this because we just had slit trenches where we went to the bathroom and we wanted something more comfortable. Our officer was thinking ahead. Instead of installing it right away, we hid the coffin in some heavy foliage. Sure enough, about three hours later this jeep came roaring in with an engineering officer who demanded that we produce the six-seater. Of course, we played innocent and acted as if we didn't know anything about it. He was steaming. He said he'd find it and bring it back. He said, "You guys will be squatting and straining over a slit trench again if I have anything to say about it!" We were smart enough to keep it hidden for four or five days while he kept swinging by with that jeep and checking us out. Finally, when we decided he had given up, the guys dug a big hole and we set up the six-seater. Naturally, we had to divide off two holes for the officers. We'd say, "They shit perfume, so they want to have their own."

There was one officer who was a nasty SOB. Of course, he used the two-seater on the officer's end. We had a guy who was sort of feeble; he was shell-shocked and one of his jobs was to take care of the latrines. His name was Lenny. He was always being bawled out by this nasty officer. To treat the latrines, Lenny had to put lime in the bottom of the trench and then pour gas in it.

One day he waited and watched for the officer who was always treating him like dirt. He poured the gas all over and he threw in a match when the guy was in there. There was a mini-explosion and the officer came out screaming, with his rear-end singed. Everyone was laughing. Of course, they caught this poor simpleton but he said he didn't know anyone was using the latrine. He had poured the gas on the far end of the GI side, but the flames shot up. He swore he didn't know anybody was in there. Of course, he gave us a little smile because he knew exactly what he was doing. We were standing there laughing hysterically. Lenny did us all a favor. We didn't have to put up with this mean SOB for a while because he was hospitalized.

We had a saying after that, though: " If you want fresh roasted nuts anytime, call Lenny." ★

Mindoro – PT Boat Racing

I was given an intelligence mission of scouting Japanese shipping. Along with one of the local natives, I was sent to the island of Verde, which was between the straits of Mindoro and Luzon. Our job was to scout the island of Mindoro and watch Japanese shipping. We boarded a PT boat with all of our gear. Then, in the wee hours of the morning, we took off. Headquarters was in communication with an Aussie who was already on Mindoro. The 19th Infantry was preparing to invade the island and we were gathering as much information as possible in a short period of time.

We slipped out as quietly as we could, with complete radio and light blackout. The PT boat slipped in about 300 to 400 yards offshore. We waited for prearranged signals from flashing lanterns on shore, and flashed back to let them know we were coming. We paddled to shore in a rubber boat and were met by two natives. The boat was going to be our escape vehicle, so we hid it, secured everything, and followed the two natives up to where we were to meet the Australian scout. All that night we set up our gear and watched the Japanese shipping with our binoculars. We could see that they were reinforcing the island. Most of the shipping was directed to Luzon, but some ships were coming in to reinforce Mindoro. The heavy shipping indicated to me that they were really reinforcing Luzon, and that's where they had decided to make their stand.

The Australian indicated to us that there had been heavy Japanese scouting parties. Evidently they had gotten suspicious that someone was spying on them from the island, probably because they picked up on radio signals. I don't think we were there more than two and a half days before the pressure became too great and we were given orders to get out. We could hear the Japanese scouting parties, and they had dogs.

We had prearranged with the PT boat how we would get out if there were problems. On the third day we decided to leave and we made contact with the boat. Our instructions were to meet them at a certain time and so many yards out from shore. They were going to make one pass, and one pass only, so we were to be prepared. They would hook us on and pull away as soon as we got out there. We left at night, got in one rubber boat and went out, taking as much equipment as we could. The Australian came with us.

We pulled out. We were flashing a flashlight to let them know where we were. The PT boat came bearing down on us, no lights. They came roaring in. We were lucky. On the first pass, they hooked onto us and we went tearing down the channel with Japanese gunboats chasing us. They were trying to pull us into the boat as we tore along. Finally they got us on board and we held on for dear life. I had my arms wrapped around the rope tie-downs. It was the wildest ride I ever had. I was more frightened then, being exposed out on the water riding at breakneck speed with Japanese gunboats chasing us down the channel, than being hunted by the Japanese. I had second thoughts, and I wished I was back on the island taking my chances, hiding under bushes. I wasn't sure if I pissed my pants or the spray from the water wet me, but I was sure glad to get the hell out of there all in one piece.

Seaside Resort - Island of Verde

They dropped us off at Goodenough Island to rest. That was an experience, too. On Goodenough Island they had their own form of entertainment. There was one jail with one cell, and in it was one Japanese prisoner. The Filipinos were so proud to have captured this guy. His eyes were black and his jaw was broken. When the Americans would come there and get drunk, they'd fight the prisoner. One night this Texan goes in the cell to take on the prisoner but the Jap ended up throwing him all over the place. He kept saying, "American sonofabitch!" That was all he could say in English.

About two and a half weeks later we invaded Mindoro. ★

Invasion of Mindoro – December 15, 1944
Living Through the Danger Zone

After we ran the gauntlet between the straits of Verde and Mindoro and we escaped back to our base, I was in for a surprise. I hadn't realized that we were assembling the division to attack Mindoro and hold that island for use as a staging ground for the attack on Luzon.

On the way to Mindoro, our invasion fleet was attacked by the first kamikaze pilots that I had seen — young Japanese pilots who would dive their planes into our ships. We were escorted by destroyers and battle cruisers and a number of air-craft carriers. The planes flew over the ships as we approached the island. They were desperately diving into us because our fire power was so strong. They came diving down, and one put a battle cruiser out of commission because it hit the control tower. The pilots were not scheduled to return to any air strip. They knew they were in the air to destroy our fleet. Their mission was a one-way ticket to hell. Of course, they believed they were going to heaven. They were the divine wind.

Again, my outfit was in the assault waves and we were the first on the beaches. We met very little resistance so we thought this was going to be a picnic. We practically waltzed in off our landing crafts. But we were there on the beach no longer than a few hours when all of a sudden one of these kamikaze planes hit one of our ammunition ships, and the ship just shot into the air. There was such a tremendous explosion that it cre-ated a tidal wave. We had to run away from the beaches because the water roared in and engulfed our positions. Some of our troops were drowned. Fortunately for me and my officer and some of the other soldiers, we had moved up into the inte-rior, so we didn't get caught in the tidal wave. Standing up on the hill looking back, it was the most impressive thing I had ever seen. I couldn't believe the size of the tidal wave that the explosion created. It was nearly 100 feet high. We couldn't see the sky when the wave came at us.

We moved inland as fast as we could, organizing ourselves to prepare for any resistance or attacks from the Japanese who were stationed on the island. Then there was panic. We were told that the Japanese navy was steaming in behind our invasion force. They were trying to put a pincer movement on us to trap us between their ground forces and the naval force that was coming in behind us. This is where I first saw PT boats in action. There were two squadrons that were sweeping in and out and firing as many torpedoes as they could to keep the Japanese force from landing. Besides the PT boats, two carriers were sending out Corsairs and just strafing and bombing everything in sight. Between the PT boats and the airplanes, they saved our asses because they prevented the Japanese from landing their force behind us. In the meantime, we were driving the Japanese ground troops back into the hills to the point where we lost contact with them. At the time it didn't seem possible, but within a few days we had secured the island with very few casualties. The casualties that we received were mostly from the tidal wave and our friendly fire.

In the meantime, the Seabees and the Air Force had set up an airfield so we could launch our planes to bomb Manila and control the straits where the Japanese had shipping lanes. After a few days my officer sent me out to see if I could make any contact with any of the Japanese. While scouting and walking along, I discovered a single-gauge railroad. My curiosity got the best of me. I thought if I could get to the end of this thing, there must be something worth spotting. I walked the railroad, but after being out for quite a few hours, I finally realized that I wasn't coming to the end of it, and I wasn't sure I was doing the right thing. I decided I had better move back and report how far I'd gone without discovering anything, and I hadn't reached the end of the line.

On the way back along the tracks, I wasn't quite as cautious as before because I felt pretty secure that there was nothing around. On a scouting mission, you can become more relaxed with more experience. Your finely honed senses become less keen. Your animal instincts and "crawly skin" relax and you're less leery of your situation. Although you know that to survive you must sustain a heightened level of fear and awareness, one cannot live on the edge forever and you become careless, less cautious. Sometimes you let your defense barriers down because you are exhausted, or from lack of sleep. Your complacency becomes your worst enemy and you are lulled into a safe zone. This is the Danger Zone. You become too relaxed and kid yourself into thinking it can't happen to me. That's when you put yourself in harm's way. You can't make a mistake. It could be your last. The Danger Zone can bring death or disaster.

I had walked back for quite a ways when I heard the roar of a plane. I looked and there came this Zero, bearing right down on me. I started to run like a maniac. There was no cover because the railroad had been cleared for quite a ways on either side. I ran as hard as I could, but I stumbled on one of the ties and fell flat on my face. As the plane came down it was firing, and I could feel every bullet hit my back. I could just feel every shot that was coming out of his guns as he flew over me. Suddenly I realized that in my panic my imagination had run away with me, because he wasn't shooting at me at all. As I walked on, I discovered that he was strafing the temporary airstrip that we had set up and I was right in line with it. He never came close to me. But I died a thousand deaths and it was another one of those pants-wetting situations. Of course, when I finally discovered that I was safe, and I wasn't the one he was shooting at, I sat there and laughed hysterically in relief.

While we were in Mindoro, some of the troops were sent up to fight in the Luzon campaign. My friend Moe Cohen was unfortunate, his battalion was sent to support some of the other units. I don't know too much about the Luzon campaign other than what Moe told me, but the fighting was heavy and he fought village to village and house to house. After a short time he was returned to the 19th Infantry and we all rendezvoused to sail off for the invasion of Mindanao. ★

Mindoro – Gunfight at the OK Corral

I was put on guard duty as corporal of the guards. This meant that I took the replacement guards around to each post to relieve the soldiers when their time was up. As I came up on my third post, there sat this guy with a side arm that his family had sent him. He was a Texan, and he had what looked like an old cowboy six-shooter. He challenged me. I had a side arm, too, and he said, "Draw!" I realized that he had been drinking some of the jungle juice and was as drunk as a skunk. He thought he was in a cowboy movie. The more I talked to him, the worse it got. I tried to calm him down, to keep him from drawing that stupid gun, because every now and then he would wave it at me. I thought for sure that he was going to blow my brains out. He kept calling me things like Snake-eye Pete, and saying, "Draw, you hombre!" Every time he went for the holster I thought sure as hell I was a dead man.

Finally, someone nearby called the officer in charge. They came with a couple of soldiers and subdued him and disarmed him. They tied him up and threw him in the drain for the rain runoff. He finally fell asleep in his drunken stupor. They just left him there all night in the drain. The officers said that would teach him a lesson.

Needless to say, we didn't see too many cowboy movies after that. ★

Just Missing a Relative

Mario Frati, the man who eventually became my brother-in-law, was a sergeant with the 67th Fighter Squadron. He was a specialist in synchronizing machine guns. He heard that my division and my regiment were in Mindoro at the air strip that was being built, and he came to see if he could find me and my outfit. But a couple of weeks had passed and we were already on our way to the invasion of Mindanao. I've always been sorry that I missed him because he was like a brother. In fact, during the rough years of the Depression, his clothes were passed down to me. It would have been so wonderful to see a familiar family face. Lucky for me, Mario made it back home and married my sister, Clara. I have always thought of him more as a brother than a brother-in-law.

P.S. I found out about his attempt to find me, after I came home. ★

Fishing Village in Mindoro

The Invasion of Mindanao –
Grief and Anger

Our invasion fleet was on the way to Mindanao when we received the news that President Roosevelt had passed away. The sadness was evident throughout the ship. It was a hot, muggy, and depressing day. No one spoke much and if you looked around, there were a lot of tear-stained faces. It was the first time that the chow line was short.

It was so hot in our bunks that I decided to sneak up on deck, wearing only my underwear. (We had strict orders to stay below.) I found a spot under a 3/4-ton truck. The night was clear and the stars were so bright, you almost felt you could touch them. The breeze felt good and I fell sound asleep. In my deep sleep something awakened me. I realized I wasn't alone. Someone was touching me, and it was strange and disturbing. Through my half-slumber, I realized I was being molested. Startled, I jerked away and struck out. I hit him in the face and he hit his head on the undercarriage of the truck. It was a sergeant from our platoon. I said to him, "What the hell are you doing!" He begged me to keep quiet. He said he didn't know what had come over him, but he lost it. He was married and had two children. He begged me not to report him.

We had been good friends and we played some sports together whenever we had the opportunity. He was from Tennessee and I didn't realize it, but he admitted to me later that he felt attracted to me. He had gone to the University of Tennessee. He didn't want this to ruin his career. We didn't have much to do with each other after this incident, other than in a professional way. Every chance he got, he always thanked me for keeping my mouth shut.

When I was wounded and discharged and at home, one day my family received a letter from him telling them the kind of person I was, how proud he was that he had met me, and that I was a special person. Inside, there was a little note directed to me, saying, "Thank you for not ruining my life." I never heard from him again. ★

Mindanao – Hand–to–Hand Combat

After our beachhead in Mindanao and being in the assault waves, we started moving into the interior. We were told to fix bayonets and charge this one particular hill to try to drive the Japanese off their position. As I reached the top of the hill, it was pretty quiet and there was very little movement because of the heavy shelling. There were a lot of dead bodies around. As I moved up, I discovered that there were openings in these caverns where the Japanese had dug gun positions into the side of the mountain. Working my way around one of these openings, all of a sudden a Jap came running out with a fixed bayonet and he lunged at me. I blocked the blow and with one lucky stroke that happened in an instant, I came across with a vertical butt shot and I caught him in the side of the head. It didn't kill him right away, but he was out.

I started looking through his pockets because I had to try to identify the division we were fighting so I could get the information to the CP. He had a sort of wallet, and when I opened it, I discovered he had a family just like mine. There was a picture with his mother and father and three siblings. The coincidence struck me. There were three boys and a girl, just like in my family. They were happy and smiling and I was thinking to myself, here I just snuffed out his life.

I tried to drag him back to one of the aid men, but the aid man said he was too far gone. I'm not so sure if he really was, but they didn't take much pleasure in trying to administer aid to the enemy. Anyway, I was very upset going through his papers. During the search for more information, I found several more pictures of his family, and other little mementos that he carried with him.

That night, talking to the chaplain, I was very upset. I was angry that I had been put in this position to take someone's life. No doubt I had killed enemy soldiers with my gunfire, but this was face to face and it became too personal. I was so angry with myself and our government – not only my own, but his government as well — for putting us both in this position. Two young boys who had never seen each other before, didn't know each other, but had to commit this terrible crime against each other. I kept telling the chaplain to repeat the commandment to me that said, "Thou shalt not kill." I am not so sure I ever got a good answer from the chaplain because to this day I can't remember any profound words, or words of encouragement, though I could see the grief in his face, also. The grief for my dilemma.

Later, when I received pictures from my own family, it brought it all back. I never found any gratification whatsoever in killing this man who was supposed to be my enemy. ★

Mindanao – Union Organizing

Tropical storms were constantly moving through during our invasion of Mindanao. I believe the monsoon season was at its peak. Our supply lines were strained. Support from the Air Corps was limited. Roadways at times were like running creeks. Supply trucks carrying ammunition got bogged down in the mud. Consequently, we had to unload the trucks and serve as pack mules. With this extra load, progress was slow. The water in some areas was above our knees and we were constantly sinking into the mud. The strain would make your legs numb. Thank God the fighting was light.

To carry boxes of ammunition, we worked in tandem and relieved each other; one would do the carrying for a few miles and then the other would take over. We had solicited the help of Filipino boys. They were young kids, 15 or 16 years old, and the powers that be convinced them they were "ammo carriers." I was next to C Company as we slogged our way up to liberate the city of Davao on the other side of the island. I had been attached to Headquarters Company.

There was a Southern officer who was one of the most prejudiced bastards I ever met over in the Islands. He called the natives "gooks." When night came, these poor young Filipinos would be digging holes as best they could in the bad weather, for the protection of the CP and other officers; then they'd be ordered out of our perimeter. At night the Japanese would be trying to break into our area, and of course these young boys would be killed. It pissed me off.

When I saw what was happening, I was furious. I befriended some of the kids, and with my knowledge of Italian and some of their pidgin Spanish and English, I made them understand that they were very valuable to us and they shouldn't allow themselves to be pushed around the way they were. I convinced them that the next morning they were not to carry the ammunition until they were allowed to stay in the perimeter where they would be safe, and they should be fed properly. It was my first experience as a union organizer.

When the sergeants ordered the boys to "saddle up," as they put it, they just sat there and pretended not to understand. They looked at me and I nodded my head and they let it be known that they wouldn't carry the ammunition unless they were treated with some respect and had some protection from the Japanese. In his frustration, the sergeant finally called the captain over. The captain threatened to kill them. They were a little bit frightened, but I gave them signals not to give in and they stood their ground. One of the sergeants spotted me and told the captain. They called me up and said, "So you're the troublemaker, you little bastard!" I told them that these kids had a right to be safe like we were, especially since they were giving us so much aid in transporting our ammunition up there.

The captain called two soldiers over and they tied my hands behind me. He threatened to have me shot in the field because I was instigating an insurrection. I told them I had nothing to do with it, it was their own doing. He said, "Don't give me that shit!" and he said something about me being a New York Yankee, and this is war and we have to do what we have to do. Not being able to keep my mouth shut, I told him, "That's inhumane! They're on our side. Why are we treating them like animals, like they're the enemy? We need them, and they need us!" One of my friends from Headquarters Company saw what was going on and found my lieutenant. He came and told the captain, "Release that man, he's not under your jurisdiction. He's under my command and he's with my intelligence group." They argued back and forth. I was standing there with my hands tied behind my back. Someone came over and untied me and he said, "Come on, let's get the hell out of here."

As I was leaving, the captain told me, "You haven't seen the last of me yet," and I gave him the finger. The captain said to me, "It isn't over yet!" When we were out of earshot my lieutenant said, "Do you have to have the last word? Couldn't you just keep your mouth shut and your hands to yourself?"

It was all worth it in my mind because from that point on the kids were allowed to stay within the perimeter and eat the same food we did. Those kids treated me like a king and even dug my foxholes for me.

This all happened many years ago. But I realized at the time that we were fighting for the democracy and freedom that our forefathers had envisioned. From what I could see, the seed of that vision hadn't even broken ground. Many of our officers and leaders weren't enlightened enough. Freedom and democracy start at home. Many people from different parts of our country wanted to control our freedom and confiscate our lives. We were fighting for something that was still only a glimmer. ★

Ambush in the Shadows – Night Mission

There is a time when the sun is setting and you are given a night mission. This is the loneliest and most fearful time – especially when it is a solo mission. Your orders are not to make contact with the enemy, but to observe and to reconnoiter the area for enemy movement. You are to note enemy position, strength, reinforcement, etc.

Sometimes your imagination runs wild. Every shadow is an ambush. The more time you spend in combat, the more tense and skittish you are. The innocence and invincibility that surround you like armor when you're young start to wear thin. You are overcome with a feeling that your luck is running out – and possibly this could be the night. Your mind plays games with you. You try to convince yourself that you could fake a report and no one will suffer for your deceit. But then you think of your comrades and the consequences of your actions if you file a fairy tale report. Your conscience takes over and regardless of what happens, you carry out your orders. The fear is heavy. But when you finally complete the mission, it feels good and you are happy.

When you report to the CP and your commanding officer, a load is off your back. The daylight hours are ahead. It's quiet time. ★

Mindanao – Monkeys and Moros
April 13, 1945

After our landing in Mindanao, once we pushed inland we were relieved by a backup regiment. It was a chance to get some rest and warm, cooked food. The cook had a monkey that was about the size of a house cat. For some reason, every time I would go by him, this monkey would act like he was attacking me. He would scream and charge me. Luckily, he was on a chain. He was nasty as hell. I wanted to kill him.

Eventually we got called back to the front lines. Because of some heavy Japanese counterattacks, we started out on a forced march. About an hour into our march, all of a sudden I felt this weight hit me. It was the damned monkey. I tried to push him away. He screamed at me and I was afraid he was going to bite me. I decided when we got through with the march, I would shoot him. He would sit on any comfortable spot on my backpack or canteen and I had to carry the extra weight. This damn monkey screamed at me every time I tried to chase him off. After the second day, I'd had enough of him. Every time we would stop for a rest period, he would harass me. He would take off and I'd think he was gone trying to find food, but as soon as we'd start marching, bam! I would feel that weight on me again. Finally, I took some rope and tied him to a tree. I thought I was rid of him, but about 20 minutes later, he was back riding on my pack. He had chewed through the rope.

What was interesting is that along the way in this part of Mindanao, there were a lot of monkeys around when there wasn't any shooting. I was hoping that somebody would adopt him and he'd stay with them. But no way. This monkey thought he was put on earth to torment me.

Now the guys were teasing me. "Baby's found a new buddy." I just couldn't seem to get rid of him. When I bedded down, I couldn't get much sleep. The second day, close to settling down, I saw a native coming by. As soon as he came near me, I told him, "I'll give you this monkey." The monkey tried to get away from me, but I knew now how to handle him and I was determined. I said, "You little bastard, I hope they throw you in a pot!"

I have to mention our experiences with the Moros, who are Filipino tribesmen. They would cut off the heads of Japanese and we used to pay them for every head they brought in. But they treated us with disdain. We would have to get off the trail when we ran into them. They would spit on the trail. They were Muslims, and to them we were infidels. We knew they worked both sides of the war. One of our guys was stupid enough to let one into our compound. We went to chow, and when we came back, we found the GI dead in his tent. ★

P.S. Some of the guys had roosters and they would hold cockfights.

Mindanao — Trying to Lose My Innocence

In Mindanao, I was constantly being teased about being a virgin. My religious background made it doubly difficult for me because, although I wanted to be a man and "one of the boys," I believed that sex was meant to be a sacred act between husband and wife. There was so much peer pressure that I eventually gave in and hopped into a jeep with four other guys who were going into a small village outside of Davao where they had been visiting a certain prostitute. The guys were teasing me all the way to Davao. I think they were more anxious for me to have my first experience than for their own adventure. I was too embarrassed to back out and I just kept my mouth shut.

We arrived at a little hut-like building and there were three little children running around outside. There was a porch, and inside the building there was an outer room with a few chairs. I could hear voices and laughter in the next room. The little kids were playing around and looking at us. Finally, a woman came out and it was my turn to go in. Her payment wasn't money, it was food. We had to give her food because she was doing this to feed her family. God only knows where her husband was.

> "Her payment wasn't money, it was food."

When I finally got in the room and got a good look at her, I realized she was pregnant. I felt awful. I felt I was dirt for even considering coming here for a few seconds of pleasure at the expense of someone who was trying to survive. She was putting her life on the line by working as a prostitute for food for her family. I was startled to see myself in a mirror, and I remember staring at myself and saying, "You don't belong here." First I gave her the food. I had brought a number of cans and I gave her everything I had. The guys had told me just to give her one, but I gave it all to her. I finally told her I couldn't do this. But I begged her to please not tell anybody when I went out. I was planning to put on an act. After a while, when I felt I could leave, I put on a big smile and told the guys how great it was.

In life you learn that lies don't pay. Her three little kids, unbeknownst to me, had peeked through the bamboo. One of them hollered out, "He chicken! He chicken!" Of course, the jig was up and I knew I had to tell the truth. I was ridiculed and laughed at all the way back to camp. To me, it was almost more painful than being wounded. I was told that I wasn't a man until I "got my rocks off." When I got back to the compound, I was ruthlessly teased and laughed at. I couldn't wait to be sent out on my next patrol.

There are many casualties of war, and to me, the wound I received that day was so deep and embarrassing that I have never forgotten it. To this day, I wonder why society ridiculed me because I wouldn't violate something that was beautiful – a mother with child. And I believed then that sex was a very precious act between husband and wife. In retrospect, I was pretty naïve about the whole thing.

Later, when I was wounded and convinced that I had lost my ability to ever experience this part of life, my perspective changed. I understood why other soldiers, knowing they might never go home, were able to do this and enjoy it. ★

Davao – May 2, 1945
Wounded Near Mandog Hill,
Mindanao – June 10, 1945

Because we were concentrating our forces on the city of Davao, which was a Japanese stronghold, we were sent out on numerous scouting missions. Japanese resistance was really very fierce. It was the monsoon season, very heavy rain. Because of the weather and the resistance and concentrations of enemy troops, we were bogged down. We had very little air activity due to the weather, so the bombing of enemy troops in their stronghold was limited. Our scouting missions were also limited, but every chance we had, we were sent out to either gather information or try to capture a Japanese soldier. Of course, we talked to the locals, too, trying to learn how many forces the Japanese had around Davao.*

One day, a naval officer showed up and I was given the assignment of getting him to a point overlooking Davao. We had American cruisers and warships out in the bay, and he was going to give us extra firepower by directing their guns on Davao. Three Filipino scouts and I led him up into this observation area where he could direct the fire. He had direct communications with the heavy cruiser. While we were sitting there and he was directing fire, somehow the Japanese traced the radio signals and they sent out their scouting parties to find us and eliminate us. A young boy from one of the nearby villages came running in to alert us that Japanese scouts were on our trail and they had dogs. We used two of the Filipino scouts to lead the officer out. I and one of the Filipinos tried to divert the enemy's attention. I kept my fingers crossed that our diversion would allow the naval officer to get away, and this young Filipino scout would lead me through some of the villages and back to our lines.

Fortunately, the rain was so heavy the dogs couldn't always follow our tracks. The Filipinos hid us in some of their huts. The Japanese were interrogating them and threatening them with bodily harm if they were concealing us. Listening and talking to some of the Filipinos, I realized that the Japanese were setting up for a counterattack because we had encircled Davao. After several sleepless nights, we finally reached our lines, went back to the CP, and I reported to my officer. I found out that the naval officer had also returned safely.

I was completely covered with mud, and one of the officers said "Good job" and told me, "Why don't you go wash?" There were shell holes there with a lot of water. First I just jumped in with all my clothes on, and tried to scrub off the mud. Then I took all my clothes off and continued to wash off as much of the dirt as I could. Suddenly, in the middle of what was a leisurely bath in the shell hole, all hell broke loose. The Japanese had some kind of buzz bombs that were very antiquated. They looked like slow-moving rockets. They weren't very effective. Here I was, stark naked. I jumped out of the shell hole, grabbed my rifle, and ran up a knoll to our outer perimeter. When I got to the top, I heard people shouting at me, but with all the firing and noise, I couldn't make out what they were saying. I found out later they were shouting because they had pulled back slightly and I ran out in front of our line without realizing it.

As I reached the top of the ridge, I went down on one knee, and noticed a field phone still attached to a tree. Maybe it was just my imagination, but I thought I could hear voices. As I got up to put the phone to my ear, a burst of machine gun fire hit me. I remember hearing the chattering of machine guns. I caught it underneath my left testicle and groin area and it smashed into my pelvis. It felt like someone had given me a blow with a baseball bat. There was dirt flying all over me from the machine gun fire. The impact from the bullets blew me back, fortunately, so that I fell on the other side of the knoll and wasn't fully exposed to enemy fire. I was still being shot at and I called out. The aid man said to lie still and they

113

would get me out. Because of the heavy fire, they brought up some light mortars and started zeroing in on the Japanese positions.

In the meantime, while I was lying in wait, I put my hand down where I was shot and discovered my whole groin area was numb. I thought they had shot all my privates away. I was so dejected and disgusted. I thought this ended everything before it ever got a chance to start. It was all over. One of the things the other soldiers would kid me about was that I was still a virgin. When they finally reached me, there were three other GIs there, and I just kept saying, "Aw, shit! Aw, shit!" They said, "What's the matter? We'll get you out of here!" I said, "Aw, shit! I can't believe it. I've never been with a girl and now I'll never know what it's like because it's gone." They started to laugh. "It's not gone. You still have everything there. You're bloody as hell, but you still have everything there." They dragged me out and they stuck morphine in my shoulder. I could no longer feel pain, everything was numb. They were trying to carry me out and we all got into a laughing jag because I'd thought everything was gone. It was just a crazy laughing jag. When

"*The impact from the bullets blew me back...*"

they finally got me down to the base of the hill, they somehow stopped the bleeding. Through the morphine, I remember being in an ambulance going down a hill. The pain from the bouncing was probably worse than the pain when I was hit.

They got me to a field hospital and I was operated on that night to remove the bullets. I was pretty much out of it for a couple of days. I talked to a priest and he helped me write a letter home to my family, telling them that I was "slightly wounded." That's the last I remember until they took me to a base hospital. From there I was shipped out to the States. ★

---

* We found out later we had killed 700 Filipinos who had sided with the Japanese.

Between Davao and Halloran General Hospital

After surgery in the field hospital, I was shipped back to a hospital in Leyte. I noticed that in our tent there were two rows of beds. On one side were the more severely wounded. On the other side were the so-called SIW (self-inflicted wound) soldiers. When I began to feel better, I observed that the wounded on the opposite side from me were not catered to or treated as nicely as we were.

I remember one soldier in particular who was from Chicago, who was in a full body cast. He kept complaining and made such a nuisance of himself that he screwed himself right out of a medical discharge. He was an SIW soldier. He complained and cried that he was always in pain. The staff tried to treat him. Finally, the doctor said they'd have to break into the cast and see what was wrong. They took X rays but couldn't find anything. They finally took the cast off and when they did, they realized he had been playing a game and they sent him back to a rehab center. The last I knew, he was going back to his outfit. The nurses usually didn't talk about other patients. The reason one of the nurses told me about this was that I was pretty quiet and I always responded that I was feeling fine. She was concerned because she saw very little activity on my part. I hadn't been out of bed since I arrived as they had me in some kind of traction.

When they removed the traction, the nurse said, "You haven't gotten out of bed yet. How do you feel?" I said I felt great, because while you're lying in bed under medication, you feel fine. She said, "Well, you know, they feel you're getting ready to go to the next center for rehab and back to your outfit." Of course, that made me happy because I thought I was healing really well. She made a comment that they wanted to see me walk, so from now on there would be no bed pan, I could walk to the john.

About an hour later I put one leg over the side of the bed and slid the other one over, pulled myself up, and as soon as I put my weight on the wounded leg, I just fell right over. They rushed over and lifted me up, and the nurse said, "What is it?" I told her, "I can't feel my leg. It feels like it's asleep and it has no feeling at all." That little nurse really knew something was wrong. She called a doctor over and he stood at the foot of my bed and talked to me. Unbeknownst to me, while he was talking he was pricking my foot and leg with a needle or pin. I never felt a thing. He told the nurse someone would be coming over to give me some tests. The next thing I knew, they were shipping me back to the States on a litter. That's when I found out that I had a femoral nerve injury.

In the meantime, back at the war, my friend Moe was busy getting shot up, too. He couldn't let me one-up him. He was sent out on a mission to capture a prisoner, to get information. There were two jeeps – Moe and his driver in one, and four men in the other. They were ambushed and he was hit in the shoulder. Another soldier was wounded, and two were killed. When they got back to their regimental headquarters, Moe reported what had happened and marked a map with the location. His sergeant, nicknamed "Kimo," knew exactly where the enemy was set up. Moe told them he wanted to go back. They then returned to the area with an officer and a platoon of soldiers and wiped out the Japanese embedded there. Back at headquarters they finally dressed Moe's wound. When it was over, Moe was awarded a Purple Heart and a bronze star in the field. I got mine later. ★

Hospital Train – August 1945

There were 50 hospitals around the country that were designated for wounded war veterans coming back from overseas. The hospitals were strategically located so the soldiers would be as close to home as possible. I was sent to Halloran General Hospital on Staten Island. After landing at an airfield in the States, special buses and trains transported us to our hospital destinations.

I recently read an article from the archives of *Newsweek* that triggered a memory of my transport experience. It mentioned patients who traveled in special cars with wire windows and military police on guard. The cars were designated for "psychoneurotic patients." I was shipped stateside from my field hospital in the Philippines in a plane specially outfitted for care of wounded soldiers. Others went on a hospital ship. We were placed on litters. Inside the plane on both sides were two tiers where our litters were stacked. In the back of the plane was something that resembled a wire cage. In the cage were two patients; one was very quiet, but the other chattered constantly. I asked a nurse why they were in there, and she told me they were "psychoneurotic patients." They had to be treated for what they referred to at that time as shell shock, what we today call post-traumatic stress disorder (PTSD). These poor bastards were looked upon with disdain. They were considered to be on the same level as the self-inflicted wound patients.

Because of the medical treatment we required, we made several stops on the way home. After leaving Leyte, we landed at Goodenough Island. We stayed overnight for treatment and refueling and then went to Kwajalein. After an overnight there, we went to Hawaii, then on to San Diego.

The regular patients were transported from the plane to the hospital by ambulance, but the so-called problem patients were brought in a paddy wagon. At every hospital where we were treated, the unfortunate men from the cages were put into something that looked like a cell. I thought it was very cruel. The caretakers would actually hose them off through the bars. One of the men was considered to be violent, but the other was docile. The way they were treated really affected me. At the hospital in Oahu, Hawaii, I was placed closer to them. The whole cell was covered with tarps, supposedly so we could sleep without them disturbing us. But one of them

The Cave*

managed to crawl to the top of the bars and started calling, "Is Chet there? Chet! Chet!" A nurse told me that Chet was one of his friends who had been killed in action. It was one of the saddest things I have ever seen. I can still hear him asking for Chet and crying.

What I learned from this experience is that man's inhumanity to man doesn't just apply to the enemy.

In contrast, today veterans are treated with kindness. Someone finally understands our problems. Our caregivers have compassion. They follow through and treat us with dignity, and make us feel that we're worth something. I think we should all be grateful that this malady is now understood. ★

---

*Prior to my VA treatment, I stayed alone in my room a lot. I was suffering emotionally from post-traumatic stress disorder (PTSD). This is an incomplete sketch I drew during that time, depicting myself in "The Cave" (my room).

Halloran General Hospital

When I was hospitalized at Halloran, I had been losing weight and was treated for hookworms. In the field hospital they had removed a bullet and classified my injury as a gunshot wound. I knew there had to be more to it because when I was wounded, all I could hear was light machine gun fire. It wasn't until I got to Halloran General Hospital that they discovered there were other metal fragments in me and a bullet lodged in my tailbone. I had been hit underneath my left testicle and somehow the bullet went through my body and lodged in my tailbone. To this day, there are metal fragments in my groin and pelvic area.

Some of the hospitalized soldiers also had psychiatric care. I was situated next to some ex-prisoners of war from Corregidor and Bataan and Japan. They were in bad shape. Their teeth were rotten and they had prematurely aged. Even though I was roughly the same age they were, I remember looking at them and thinking how much older they looked.

These ex-prisoners who had been shipped to Japan as POWs said they were lucky because they were placed in factories to work and once they were with the civilians, the civilians treated them well. In fact, the civilians were mistreated by the military as much as the American soldiers were, and they feared the military as much as we did. We had some long talks about the Japanese people and many of them said they liked the civilians. They just hated the Japanese military. It's an interesting thing. Wherever the people were working, the military enforcers used to walk up and down with canes. If they felt the people were slacking in their support of the war effort, the civilians would get just as much of a beating as the GIs.

While I was at Halloran, Moe Cohen's brother was a student at NYU. He came up to Halloran to see me and brought me a box of candy. Being so far from home, it was great to see my "extended family." Moe was a dear friend. Even then, he thought of me.

119

A girl from Juilliard School of Music was a hospital volunteer, and she used to sing to me. She was a soprano and she would come in all dressed up and sing *Jealousy* and other songs. I sensed that she liked me but because I was confined to bed care, there was no way I could get to go out on a date with her.

Much later during my recovery when I could move around, there was a WAC, Irene, whom I did take out on a date. She treated me with such kindness. I was sorry that we didn't keep

Halloran Hospital

in touch because I actually had a little bit of the flutters for her. She was the first girl who paid so much attention to me. She was there all the time.

We had Italian and German prisoners who worked in the wards. The Italian prisoners were like us. They were friendly and happy and some of the nurses even had affairs with them. Some were really handsome men. But the German prisoners never forgot they were Nazis. If they thought no one was looking, they would spit on the floor. They were so arrogant and nasty with us that they had to be watched all the time. They were only allowed in the ward to do the heavy work. The Italian prisoners had a free hand in the hospital and could wander freely. The German prisoners were restricted to the grounds. They did most of the heavy work because they didn't particularly like to have contact with us. Some of them would go by the wards of patients who were burned, poor guys who were caught in burning tanks. If the Germans heard them crying and screaming, they would smile and talk to each other. It didn't endear them to me. ★

Where are the Wacs?

Fort Niagara – Malaria and AWOL

On my first weekend pass from the hospital, I went home to Rochester. The second day home I got a very high fever and shakes. I realized I was having a malaria attack. Someone called the Red Cross, and they made arrangements for an ambulance to come from Fort Niagara and take me to the hospital there. I was there about a week.

Unfortunately, they weren't equipped to take in malaria patients and the only disease ward they had with an available bed was a VD ward. So I was put there. The nurses didn't treat people in that ward very kindly. The patients were expected to get up and wash the latrines and take care of their own cleaning, because no one figured they were that sick. I, on the other hand, was very sick with a high fever. The day after I arrived, the morning nurse said, "Come on, get up, it's your turn to clean latrines." I looked at her in a daze. She kept trying to push me and she was very insulting. She said, "If you think you're going to lie around here on your ass without pulling your share of the load, you're wrong!" She told me, "When you play, you pay." I told her to get the hell out of my room and she started pulling off my covers. I took a pitcher of water and threw it at her. Of course, I had a 104° fever. At the time of the commotion, the doctor came in and told her, "Don't you read the charts? This patient has malaria. He's from Halloran General Hospital! You treat him with a little more empathy." After that, I didn't have a problem; I was relieved of latrine duty.

"She told me, when you play, you pay."

The most embarrassing part of my stay was when my parents came to visit me. They told my parents what ward I was in and at the entrance to the ward in the biggest block letters you ever saw, was a sign that read **VD WARD.** Knowing my mother, I'm sure she almost died of embarrassment. When she came in, she didn't even want to hug me or touch me. I felt rather sad that she didn't come near me until I realized why she was staying away from me. Then I explained that this was the only ward with an available bed. The doctor came in and explained to her that this was the only disease ward they had, and because there were a lot of prostitutes around Niagara Falls, the guys would catch VD.

On the day I was discharged from the hospital, I went home and told my family that I had 30 days' leave. Actually, I was still technically on "active duty," so I went AWOL for a month. When I went back to Halloran, the MPs picked me up in Grand Central Station as AWOL. I don't know how they knew I was on that train. They might have been there to pick up other GIs and found me. I was on crutches, and the people in the train station were all telling the MPs, "Leave that little boy alone!" I was actually put in a lockup. The next morning they let me out and I got bawled out because I was scheduled for surgery. They said it was a good thing I came back when I did, because there was a Colonel Croce who came in from Walter Reed Hospital in Washington just to perform the surgery on me. He was going to remove the bullet from the base of my spine. They told me that if I hadn't gotten back, after he made the trip up to Halloran, they were going to toss me in the clink and throw away the key. Of course, that was all bluster.

The surgery proved to be very successful. I avoided having to put up with a temporary colostomy although I couldn't eat for nearly a month. They fed me liquids and IVs and put me in lateral traction on my stomach. ★

Christmas at Halloran — 1945

It was the Christmas and New Year's holidays. I had just had surgery. Consequently, I was restricted to my ward. Everyone who didn't need immediate medical treatment or could manage to get out went home for the holidays, sometimes accompanied by nurses. This was my first holiday in the States after three years in the service. In fact, that morning one of the New York newspapers had taken my picture and I was on the front page. They brought in telephone operators so I could call home. That was their way of compensating me. My Christmas present for being stuck in the hospital. I did have an occasional visitor. One of them, a compassionate student from Pratt Institute, came to Halloran and sketched my picture. Her name was Beatrice.

One of the nurses who was on duty thought I was looking rather sad and she told me not to worry. She said, "We'll have our own little celebration. I'll get all dressed up for you and we'll have some fun." She was my night nurse and we called her Goldie. She was Jewish and had volunteered for duty so others could have time off. So on New Year's Eve, she came in all dressed up. She was a blonde, and I can still remember that low-cut cranberry dress. She had a bottle of champagne. That was my first taste of champagne. Of course, it gave me a bit of a buzz.

Goldie was drinking pretty freely, and we were having a wonderful time. It was my first experience of lovemaking. The first time I'd ever felt a woman's breasts and thighs. She tried to maneuver on top of me, even though I was in lateral traction. At that point my intentions were not so honorable. I just wanted my first screw. I won't go into the details, but somehow I managed to get out of my lateral traction and I still had a catheter in me. Before the evening was over, I was rushed to one of their emergency areas so I could get sewed up again because I was bleeding. There was a bit of panic but there was a great smile on both

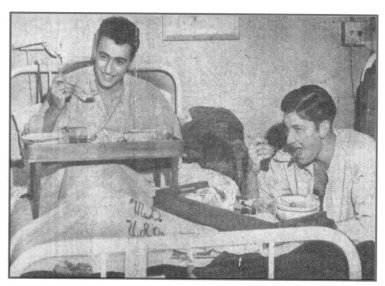

NEW YORK TIMES: STUFFING... Even though confined to bed, Pfc. David Mancini, of Rochester, N.Y., gets his fill of turkey in Halloran General Hospital. With him is Pfc. Charles Amero, of Essex, Mass.

of our faces. Not that I actually "did" anything. She was just very kind and nice to me and I was trying to play the part of a lover, but I'm afraid I was a little too inexperienced. When we went into emergency, the surgeon said, "What the hell happened here?" Goldie smiled. He looked at her and saw how she was dressed and she responded, "We've just been a little too naughty."

The next morning she came to see me and told me she was being transferred. She said, "You know, Davey, it was all worthwhile just to see that smile on your face and that little silly grin that you had." She wished me luck and gave me a hug and a kiss and said she would drop me a line. She did, and we kept in contact for a while. The last time she wrote to me she was getting married to someone from Buffalo.

It was during my stay at Halloran that I stopped going to church. I'd always been very religious, and church had been a part of my life. But one Sunday I went to church and they were preaching against Russia and ranting about the threat of the communists. I'd just gotten through with all this killing, and here they were talking about Russia. I turned my wheelchair around and left.

Ultimately, my surgery proved a success and after a few months of rehabilitation, I was finally discharged. When I was finally discharged I was so happy to get home, but I struggled with a striking realization – I went to war and I lost my God. To this day I am not quite sure whether I'll ever believe. But I'm trying real hard. ★

The Alcohol Cure...Celebration in Manhattan

The day the war ended, I was returning to Halloran General Hospital from Rochester, where I had gone on a weekend pass. In Manhattan I met a fellow soldier who was also recovering from his wounds. I was on crutches, and his arm was in a cast mounted on a brace that held his arm out from his body. To reach Halloran we took the Staten Island Ferry. The celebration was incredible. Fire boats were shooting water plumes into the air; the bells and ships' whistles and sirens were deafening. On the ferry we met a mother traveling with her twin daughters, who appeared to be about 16 years old. The mother hugged us and told the kids, "Go over and kiss those poor boys." They did – very tender, shy, and gentle kisses. We learned that she had a son who was a soldier and she was delighted and relieved that he would soon be coming home. When the ferry docked, she insisted that we come with her to her apartment for coffee. We were grateful for the gesture and agreed. I never even got her name. It was just one of those wonderful moments of camaraderie that you share. By the time we finished our coffee and visit, we had missed our bus to the hospital, so she had a relative drive us. At Halloran, people were going crazy with joy. The world around us was in a total frenzy. The next day those of us who were ambulatory celebrated again because we received a special three-day pass. I decided to go home again.

That trip to Rochester launched me on a little adventure that I'll never forget. I headed back to Grand Central Station and purchased my train ticket. Since I was an hour early, I decided to kill some time by walking around. I was on crutches, but I wandered around the station area looking at all the debris from the previous night. From the aftermath, I knew the party in Manhattan must have been tremendous. Some of the revelers were still staggering around. I leaned against a building to rest a bit and enjoy the fact that I was feeling pretty good about the whole thing. I was going home, the war was over, and it felt great. A woman who looked to be in her late 30's came along. She was a sight. War paint an inch thick. Her mascara and bright red lipstick were smeared, and she looked like she'd had a busy time welcoming the soldiers back. She spotted me leaning there on my crutches and rushed over, reaching out to me. "Oh, you poor boy, you poor boy," she kept saying, and she kissed me. She had a grip on me and I couldn't get away from her. She was kissing me on the mouth and hugging me, and she smelled of booze. I was horrified. Finally, she let go and asked me where I was going. I told her I was on my way home and I had to catch my train.

> *"This woman had given me a disease, even though she meant well..."*

I was scared to death. Every chance the Army had, they showed us pictures of the effects of VD and stressed that we had to be really careful because we could get it from prostitutes or "street women." The movies we had seen were so grotesque, they made me nauseous. I was a young kid, still a virgin, very impressionable, and I thought sure as hell I was done for. This woman had given me a disease, even though she meant well. I was desperate, thinking I might be taking a disease home and possibly transmitting it to my family. What would my mother think of me? I was fighting demons in my mind.

Looking up and down the street, I spotted a drug-store that was open. I went in and bought cotton swabs and alcohol. Now I had to find a place where I could clean myself. I found a little coffee shop, went in, and asked for the restroom. I locked myself in a stall and wiped my face, my lips, my neck, and my hands with the alcohol, trying to

clean away the germs. In my feverish anxiety, I was
convinced I had to clean my penis, too, because probably
I'd picked up a disease from
that crazy lady. So, without
thinking twice, I started washing
my penis with the alcohol. Holy
shit! I thought I'd go into orbit.
The pain was excruciating.
Later on, as I thought about it, I
was certain the alcohol would've

> *He looked at me and started to smile. He said, "Davey, I think you need to get laid."*

killed any germs or disease… and probably my penis, too!
That was the second time around. The bullets missed it, but
the alcohol didn't!

All the way home I kept thinking about the disease
I'd probably contracted. I was so concerned, I wasn't sure if
I should hug or kiss my parents. I didn't know what I
should do. When I got home I kept everybody at arm's
length, but I knew I had to talk to someone. I was close to
my Uncle Pete. He was a bachelor and was known around
town as quite a ladies' man. I figured I could confide in him.
"Uncle Pete, do you think I'm going to be all right? Do you
think I've done the right thing by using the alcohol?" He
looked at me and started to smile. He said, "Davey, I think
you need to get laid." He convinced me that I had retained
my innocence. I had spent the last three years dodging not
only bullets but VD, too. ★

The War Comes to Haunt Me Once Again

Approximately three months after being discharged, I had another episode with my wounds. I was out on a date when my leg wound started oozing blood and puss. I'd had pain and redness around the groin area for about two weeks. My friend drove me over to my family doctor, who closed and dressed the wound. He recommended that I go to the VA. They immediately sent me to Highland Hospital. The next day they operated and removed the shell of a tracer bullet.

My friend Moe Cohen and my family came to see me almost every day. Of course, Moe was up to his old tricks. One night he came to visit me with his girlfriend, Annabelle (now his wife). When visiting hours were over he said goodnight, but then he grabbed the foot of my bed and dragged me out into the hall. I said, "What are you doing?" He said, "Never mind, Davinko." Before I knew what was happening, my bed was standing in the hallway by the elevator. Annabelle was asking, "Are you crazy?" Moe answered, "No, no, no! He's supposed to be out here to greet all the people coming off the elevator!" Moe shepherded Annabelle onto the elevator and waved. "Have a good evening, Davinko!" He left me there in the hallway. Some nurses went by and asked me what I was doing there. They had a good chuckle, and brought me back to my ward. After another 28 days of hospitalization, I was discharged once again.

> "The war was over, the world was on its way to recovery, and I was healing along with it."

The war was over, the world was on its way to recovery, and I was healing along with it. ★

Epilogue

The diary you have just read is my father's story of his experience as a World War II combat veteran. This story is not fiction, nor is it a television series or a Hollywood movie. This is the real deal. And unlike a Hollywood movie where the actors killed in action get up, leave the set, and return home to their families and friends, many of the "players" in this story never go home unless it's in a body bag. And the civilians, including children, who are caught in the crossfire or bombing raids, are not extras on the Hollywood set. When they die, it's for real. The blood is real. Families are destroyed – children become orphans – and some will never see another birthday.

Many soldiers on both sides, and civilians as well, survive the war only in the sense that they are still alive. Many are scarred for life, physically and emotionally. If you ever want to see the permanent scars on the veterans of World War II, Korea, and Vietnam, stop by a Veterans Administration Office and meet some of the people we call heroes. Ask them if they think they are heroes. I can speak for my father as I have seen the remorse he feels for what he had to do. I have seen him cry 50 years later about the young lives he had to snuff out in order to survive. These were young men with families just like his.

A very good friend of mine once said, "I didn't become a man until I learned how to cry." Just the opposite of the macho image our society projects, isn't it? I would say that if anyone takes another person's life and does not cry about it, there is something wrong.

A friend once told me that his cousin was a cadet at West Point Military Academy. I asked him what his cousin was learning at West Point. My friend remarked that his cousin was learning how to kill people. I responded, "But isn't he also taking academic classes and learning skills that will even-tually help him to get a good job?" My friend replied, "Yes, he is, but he's still learning how to kill people." And now that I think about it, if the young cadets are learning how to kill, they must be learning how to hate as well. For how could you kill someone you love?

In this country we call it defense, but it's really offense. And I'm not talking about a football game. I read a quote recently that said, "Americans are good at killing." We could also say that the Germans and the Japanese were good at killing. So was Saddam Hussein and his regime and so are many other nations. In fact, we could probably say that the majority of mankind is good at killing. It's pretty sad, isn't it?

If you have read this entire diary and are not brought to tears, perhaps your heart has been hardened and desensitized by the United States' war propaganda machine and a false sense of patriotism. I'm not sure patriotism is such a good thing when it results in destroying the lives of other people as well as the lives of American soldiers.

Speaking of patriotism, I would like to share some final thoughts about my father. My father does not consider himself a hero. Heroes do not have nightmares and cry about what they did. I don't think very many combat veterans actually do think of themselves as heroes. You see, a hero is not someone who achieves a particular goal by killing and destroying the lives of other people. A hero is someone who can achieve the same goal without killing anyone – without the shedding of one drop of blood. A hero sees all life as precious, has compassion for all mankind, and is a master of diplomacy.

Even though my father does not consider himself to be a hero, I consider him to be a hero. But not for the same reasons that we as a society call people heroes. My dad is a hero because he has compassion for all people and he mourns the loss not only of his friends and all of the American soldiers who were killed in World War II, but he also mourns the loss of all the young Japanese soldiers who were killed, as well as the civilians – mothers, fathers, little girls and boys.

My dad is a hero because he has the courage to speak out against war. He has been there and he knows that war is ugly and is a very barbaric, inhumane, and ignorant method of settling disputes. I say ignorant because I do not believe that intelligent people would be ignorant enough to go to war. War is a terrible tragedy. I suspect that if more people experienced what my father did, they would feel the same way.

From my perspective, my father is an example of the true meaning of patriotism. First, patriotism to his own country because he does not want to see any of our young people killed or experience what he did. And secondly, not just patriotism to his own country, but to all of mankind – to all of God's creation. He has love and compassion for all people. He is a true hero.

We often hear the peculiar oxymoron "We're fighting for peace." This never really made any sense to me. You see, war and peace really begin in the hearts of men. And until the hearts of men are changed, there will never be peace on this earth.

David Mancini, Jr.